The Language of Law

The Language of Law

Andrei Marmor

OXFORD
UNIVERSITY PRESS

OXFORD
UNIVERSITY PRESS

Great Clarendon Street, Oxford, OX2 6DP,
United Kingdom

Oxford University Press is a department of the University of Oxford.
It furthers the University's objective of excellence in research, scholarship, and education by publishing worldwide. Oxford is a registered trade mark of Oxford University Press in the UK and in certain other countries

First Edition published in 2014

Published in the United States of America by Oxford University Press
198 Madison Avenue, New York, NY 10016, United States of America

British Library Cataloguing in Publication Data
Data available

Library of Congress Control Number: 2013957962

ISBN 978–0–19–871453–8

For Beth

Acknowledgments

In working on this project over the years, I have been helped by many colleagues and friends. A particular debt of gratitude I owe to Scott Soames; without his help and collaboration, in teaching, co-editing a collection on this topic, and comments on earlier drafts, I would not have managed to complete this project. I am also grateful to Gideon Yaffe, Joseph Raz, Robyn Carston, Alon Harel, David Enoch, Scott Altman, and Hrafn Asgeirsson for their comments on some earlier drafts of this work.

The book incorporates, though mostly in substantially revised form, some of my earlier publications on language and the law. In chapter 2, I used, with significant revisions, some parts of my earlier paper on the topic "Can the Law Imply More than It Says?" in Marmor & Soames, eds., *Philosophical Foundations of Language in the Law* (Oxford, 2011), ch. 5. Chapter 3 is a slightly revised version of "Truth in Law," in Freeman & Smith, eds., *Law and Language: Current Legal Issues* (Oxford, 2013), 45. In chapter 4, I used parts of a contribution I wrote for Sartor et al., eds., *Handbook of Legal Reasoning and Argumentation* (Springer, 2014). Chapter 6 is a revised version of my contribution to a symposium issue on constitutional interpretation, published in *Fordham Law Review* (82 Fordham L Rev (2013), 577).

Contents

Introduction

There is hardly any aspect of our lives that is not regulated by law in one way or another. The legal domain is vast in quantity and varied in sources. In every modern legal system there is a huge amount of regulation—constitutional, statutory, administrative, and judicial—that aims to guide our conduct, in various capacities or roles we occupy, and for a great variety of purposes. Most of this vast amount of legal content is a direct result of enactments by legal authorities. And there is only one way in which authorities can convey the legal content they aim to introduce: by communicating in a natural language. Language is to lawyers what a piano is to the pianist: the tool of her trade. Some may use it better than others, but none can conduct their business without it. The main purpose of this book is to show that a better understanding of the tool, language in the legal case, may help us to a better understanding of the trade, that is, of how the law works and how legal directives can convey the kind of legal content they aim to convey.

There is nothing new, of course, about a philosophical interest in language in the legal context. The analytical tradition in jurisprudence has always regarded philosophy of language as an integral part of legal philosophy—and not only for the simple reason that a better understanding of linguistic communication may help us to a better understanding of legal regulation. For many decades, philosophy of language has been seen as playing a foundational role in philosophy of law, underscoring its main method, as it were, the ways in which we go about doing philosophy of law itself. But this is not what I aim to do in this book. I want to put philosophy of language to a more modest and limited use, one that is focused on linguistic communication as a means of conveying legal content. Let me use a very brief historical survey to explain this difference.

H. L. A. Hart, the forebear of the analytical tradition in jurisprudence, was quite explicit about his view that philosophy of language played a foundational role in his theory of law. But what exactly that role is remained somewhat unclear and controversial over the decades that followed the publication of his seminal work, *The Concept of Law*. Both the title of his book, and the dominating views about philosophy at the time, gave the impression that Hart regarded philosophy of law as a form of conceptual analysis, and aimed to articulate the concept of law and related concepts that play a central role in law, such as the concept of a rule, or a legal obligation and the like. Hart wrote *The Concept of Law* when the so-called ordinary-language analysis, led by Wittgenstein, Austin, and Ryle, dominated the philosophical scene at Oxbridge. These philosophers held the view that most philosophical problems arise from conceptual confusions, and that careful and nuanced analysis of concepts is the main tool philosophers have to avoid those confusions and make some philosophical progress.

Concepts were not viewed as abstract objects or things of any kind. Rather, concepts stand for the myriad ways, or "functionings," as Ryle called them,[1] in which words are used by competent speakers of a natural language in a given setting or "language game." Philosophers tried to articulate the ways in which the use of words/concepts play specific roles in making moves within an interlocking set of other concepts and arguments. To be sure, they were not looking at a set of necessary and sufficient conditions for the use of concepts. Rather, ordinary-language philosophers were looking at piecemeal examination of families of conceptual connections, and ways in which the functioning of a word is dependent on the functioning of others. Furthermore, the assumption was that conceptual connections are epistemically transparent, and should be evident to any competent user of the language in question. Because we know the meaning of the words we use as competent members of the linguistic community, we should be struck with the undeniable correctness of any genuine conceptual connection whenever presented to us by the relevant philosophical elucidation.

There is no doubt that, in some respects, Hart shared these views and saw himself as working in the tradition of his peers at Oxford at the time. However, it is far from clear how much of his work in philosophy of law is, actually, a form of conceptual analysis. There

[1] *Dilemmas*, 32.

is not much of it in *The Concept of Law*. In only a handful of places in the book, Hart actually engages in anything that can be seen as analysis of concepts or conceptual connections. As I argued elsewhere at some length, most of *The Concept of Law*, and Hart's legal philosophy in general, is concerned with the possibility of reduction. The main question for Hart was whether law, and our shared understandings of what law is, can be fully reduced to facts of a nonnormative kind. Hart's theory of law is essentially a reductionist account of law, aiming to show that the legal phenomena can be fully explained by social facts—facts about how people behave, the kind of beliefs they share about their conduct, and attitudes that tend to accompany those beliefs. Whether this reductionist project can succeed is controversial, of course, but as I argued elsewhere, I do not think there is much by way of conceptual analysis grounding it.[2]

The irony, or perhaps the source of some of the confusion, is that by the time *The Concept of Law* gained worldwide recognition in the early 1960s,[3] the ordinary-language analysis in philosophy began to lose some of its appeal. Significant advances in philosophy of language, building on earlier foundational work by Frege and Russell, started to replace the interest in Wittgenstein-style analysis of conceptual connections. Philosophers became interested in the more ambitious project of constructing a theory of meaning for natural language. The aim was to provide a general theory of what meaning consists in, how it is related to truth, and how language relates to the reality it aims to represent.[4] Davidson's truth-conditional semantics, Putnam's theory of natural kind predicates, and, more generally, the interest in the possible connections between language, truth, and reality, became the more exciting philosophical projects in philosophy of language and, in a way, they spilled over to jurisprudence as well. Nevertheless, the widely shared conception (or misconception, in my view) that analytical legal philosophy is, essentially, an attempt to elucidate the concept of law

[2] See my *Philosophy of Law*, ch. 2, and "Farewell to Conceptual Analysis (in Jurisprudence)."

[3] *The Concept of Law* was published in 1961, but it was written earlier; as we know from numerous sources, Hart worked on a draft of the book during the early 1950s but waited years (some say until after Austin's death) to publish it.

[4] The interest in a general theory of meaning did not start in the 1960s, of course; the foundational work in semantics goes back to Frege and Russell decades earlier. What happened in the late 1960s–1970s is, in a way, a resurgence of these grand theoretical ambitions, largely ignoring the later Wittgenstein anti-theory stance, and pushing aside the conceptual analysis type of philosophy that marked the Oxbridge tradition of the 1940s and 1950s.

and related legal concepts, lingered in the jurisprudential tradition for decades.[5] The advances in general theories of meaning, and particularly the connection between semantics and metaphysical realism (or anti-realism), has been employed by legal philosophers as an additional and more sophisticated tool for articulating theories about what the concept of law is and how it relates to metaphysical aspects of the normative domain. Putnam's theory of natural kinds proved particularly alluring, paving the way for legal philosophers to argue that some version of natural law can be grounded in a realist–semantic analysis of the meaning of "law" and related concepts. And then, of course, Hart's legal positivism was recast in terms of an opposing semantics, sometimes labeled conventionalism or criterial semantics, holding the view that it makes no sense to understand the concept of law on the basis of an externalist semantic theory, as if the word "law" designates some normative reality out there, irrespective of people's beliefs about the true nature of its reference.[6]

The semantic interest in law, and the perception of legal philosophy as necessarily a form of conceptual analysis, persisted even in the face of Dworkin's famous critique of this method, beginning in the 1980s. In *Law's Empire*, Dworkin argued that, in spite of Hart's explicit denials, the only way to understand his conceptual analysis is to see it as an attempt to define what the word "law" means for the linguistic community that uses it, and that conceptual analysis is essentially a semantic theory, aiming to elucidate the meaning of "law." Furthermore, Dworkin argued that Hart's analysis of law actually assumes a particular type of semantic theory, one that ties the meaning of words to some established or widely shared criteria for their correct use by members of the linguistic community in question. Dworkin claimed that this semantic project is hopelessly misguided, as it would be incapable of explaining how lawyers and judges, whose concept of "law" the theory purports to elucidate, actually have no such shared concept in mind. In fact, they explicitly disagree, often quite profoundly, about what the appropriate concept is, and certainly disagree about what would constitute the criteria for its correct use.[7]

[5] To this day, actually. See for example, S. Shapiro, *Legality*; ch. 1, J. Raz, *Between Authority and Interpretation*, 62–76.

[6] See, for example, M. Moore, "The Semantics of Judging." For more references and my own stab at this realist semantics of law, see my *Interpretation and Legal Theory* (revised 2nd ed.), ch. 5.

[7] See R. M. Dworkin, *Law's Empire*, ch. 1.

The reactions to Dworkin's critique of conceptual analysis in jurisprudence were fierce and sometimes dismissive.[8] There was a widely shared sense that Dworkin assumed a very simplistic view of the connections between meaning and definitions on the one hand, and between the meaning of words and what concepts are on the other. Hart never attempted to define what "law" means, critics pointed out, because it is not what conceptual analysis purports to do. More importantly, critics argued that criterial semantics is much more sophisticated than Dworkin had taken it to be, and that it can easily explain the kind of theoretical disagreements about the law that Dworkin alluded to. In short, the main reaction to Dworkin's critique of semantic theories of law was to defend the method of conceptual analysis by way of relying on more sophisticated semantic theories and a more nuanced approach to the relations between meaning and use.

My interest in this book, however, is not about the concept of law, and certainly not about the conditions of legal validity. The methodological question that interested Dworkin and his critics (including myself at the time), of whether language plays a foundational role in the kind of philosophy we do when trying to articulate the nature of law, is something that I will not discuss in these pages. My interest here is confined to the linguistic aspects of legal directives. Whatever else law may be, and whatever the criteria of legal validity one may favor, there is little doubt that a great part of legal content is determined by authoritative directives of legislatures, judges, administrative agencies, and the like. Whether there is more to law than authoritative directives, and the questions of what determines who is a legal authority and why, are complex issues that I have discussed elsewhere.[9] My aim in this book is to examine the boundaries between linguistic and normative considerations in the inference to legal content of statutory law, and to articulate how the linguistic determinants work, without relying on any particular theory about the nature of law, or the nature of legal philosophy, for that matter.

Philosophy is in flux, of course, and paradigms shift every few decades. The focus on theories of meaning in philosophy of language has given way, in the last few decades, to a considerably broader approach, driven by an increasing realization that pragmatic aspects of

[8] I should not exclude myself from this trend. See my *Interpretation and Legal Theory* (revised 2nd ed.), 3–8. See also J. Raz, *Between Authority and Interpretation*, ch. 2.

[9] See my *Philosophy of Law*, ch. 1–4.

communication play a much greater role in our use of language than previously thought. I am not suggesting that there is a consensus among philosophers of language about the role of pragmatic determinants of linguistic communication; in fact, even the boundaries between semantics and pragmatics are contested and debated. But there is an increasing awareness that semantic theories, sophisticated and illuminating as they may have become, are just not going to suffice to explain how people manage to convey a great deal of communicated content in their everyday linguistic interactions. Contextual knowledge shared by parties to the conversation, norms governing their mutual expectations, and sometimes other local and context-sensitive factors, are essential ingredients in the inference to communicated content on an occasion of speech. Semantics and syntax are, of course, essential vehicles of communication; their features enable and constrain what people can say to each other, but they are rarely sufficient to determine what has been actually communicated. Furthermore, as Kent Bach reminds us,[10] even when a speaker intends to convey exactly what his expression literally means, and nothing else, the speaker's intention of doing so is partly what determines what his expression conveys on that occasion of speech (after all, he could have said the same thing ironically or in jest, or merely as a hypothetical in a philosophy class). In short, an increasing interest in pragmatic (and speech-act) aspects of linguistic communication marks the last few decades in philosophy of language.

My purpose in this book is to employ some of these recent advances in philosophy of language to elucidate some key aspects of legal communication, mostly in the context of statutory law. At the same time, I hope to show that some of the unique features of communication in the legal domain—in particular, its strategic nature—can be employed to put some pressure on certain assumptions in philosophy of language, enabling a more nuanced picture of how semantic and pragmatic determinants of communication work in complex and large-scale systems such as law.

Since it is the main assumption of this book that we can make some philosophical progress by paying close attention to the kind of speech act that legal enactments are, and how they determine the content of the enacted law, the assumption that legislation is a speech act needs to be substantiated. The defense of this rather commonsensical assumption

[10] See, for example, K. Bach, "Context *ex Machina*" at 27.

forms the topic of the first part of chapter 1. The second part goes on to lay down the foundations of what communicated content might consist in, focusing on what the law says or asserts. In chapter 2, I turn to the availability of implicated content, examining the possible roles of conversational implicatures and utterance presuppositions in statutory law. The main argument of chapter 2 consists in the idea that the strategic nature of legal communication calls into question the reliability of implicated content in the law. I will try to show that both the legislatures and the courts have an interest in maintaining a certain level of uncertainty about the normative framework that governs their conversation, which allows them, at least sometimes, to manipulate content that may have been implicated but not quite asserted.

Chapter 3 takes up a familiar question, but one that has strangely received very little attention in the literature—namely, whether legal directives have any truth-evaluable or propositional content. The answer to this question is of crucial importance to our ability to explain the idea of legal inferences. If laws have no propositional content, if their communicated content is not truth-apt, then the very possibility of a legal inference becomes doubtful. Inferences must take propositions as their premises. Thus, in chapter 3, I employ a speech-act analysis to show that legal directives do have truth-evaluable content. I also deal with some structural aspects of legal inferences, drawing on some analogies with David Lewis's work on truth in fiction, to show that law is one of those cases in which, under certain conditions, the saying so makes it so.

Thus, the first three chapters set up the main theoretical framework that I suggest about the role of language in the law. The next three chapters aim to apply this framework, and the limits it sets, to some particular legal controversies, mostly in the context of statutory interpretation. Chapter 4 is devoted to the issue of vagueness in the law. I argue that vagueness of legal language comes in different forms, and those engender different kinds of normative considerations that should be brought to bear on the judicial resolution of borderline cases of vague statutory terms. The issue of vagueness in law demonstrates very nicely how linguistic and normative considerations are closely entangled in the legal context, but also how important it is to keep them separate when possible. In other words, some conclusions about the content of the law follow from linguistic considerations, but not all, and often not the important ones. Vagueness and similar linguistic indeterminacies we find in legal language demonstrate some important limits of linguistic considerations in statutory interpretation. I try to show how those limits are drawn and how they might affect the different kinds of normative considerations called for.

In chapter 5, I turn attention to a particular theory of statutory interpretation, called *textualism*, which has gained considerable influence in recent years. Textualism is particularly interesting in the context of a linguistic analysis of statutory law because it purports to be based on it. Textualism urges judges to interpret the law only according to what the lawmakers have actually communicated by their enactment, eschewing any reliance on legislative intent and legislative purposes. In this chapter, I argue that some of the main insights of textualism are important, and assume a very sensible view about the determinants of law's assertive content, along the lines we explored in chapter 1. However, by building on the lessons we learned in chapters 2 and 4, we will come to see that textualism is not nearly as helpful a theory of statutory interpretation as its proponents claim. The general lesson here is similar to the lesson we learn from examining the role of vagueness in statutory language—namely, that linguistic determinants are important in shaping some of the questions that arise in statutory interpretation, but they are rarely sufficient for providing the answers.

A similar lesson, and more strikingly so, emerges in the context of constitutional interpretation. In chapter 6, I examine the role of the distinction between general evaluative concepts and their possible conceptions in the context of constitutional interpretation. The chapter presents two possible semantic models for understanding the *concept versus conceptions* distinction, arguing that neither of them is quite adequate to the task. By putting some pressure on the relations between the semantics and pragmatics of general evaluative concepts that we find in constitutional documents, I try to show that the main debates about constitutional interpretation cannot be detached from their underlying moral–political dimension. Before we can form any views on how to understand the language of general concepts deployed in constitutional documents, we must first form a view about the nature of the discourse that the constitution establishes, and views about the nature of the discourse crucially depend on the moral legitimacy of constitutionalism.

By focusing on the linguistic aspects of communication in law I hope to make some progress. But progress in philosophy is achieved in very small steps. I use some tools, borrowed from philosophy of language, to try to shed light on some of the questions that arise in the context of legal interpretation. Along the way, I hope to show that in using such tools in the legal context, we may need to reexamine the tools themselves, and I suggest some modifications of them in light of the unique context that constitutes communication in law. It would be foolish, however, to assume that any one tool, fancy and useful as it may be, can solve all of the problems. They say that if you only have a hammer, everything begins to look like a nail. I certainly hope that I do not make this mistake. Philosophy of language is a very useful tool for an analysis of statutory law, but it is only one instrument, with limited availability, and part of what I aim to show here is precisely those limits.

1

What Does the Law Say?

There are many ways in which laws can be made. Legislatures enact laws according to some prescribed procedures; judges render legal decisions in a court of law, which sometimes creates new law or modifies existing law; and countless administrative agencies issue regulations according to the authority assigned to them by statute. In this book, I will take the fairly simple view that all of these lawmaking acts are *speech acts*, and that we may gain some insights and can make some philosophical progress by carefully examining what kind of speech acts they are and how they determine the content of the law. Whatever else we might want to say about the enactment of a law, I take it as no more than common sense that it is an instance of communication, whereby the legislature (or the relevant agency or the court) communicates a certain content that it aims to enact as the new law. Common sense, however, has never stood in the way of philosophical arguments. Mark Greenberg, for example, argues that "[l]egislation uses language to make law… [but in] doing so neither requires communication nor is well understood on the model of communication…Legislatures need not intend to communicate anything by enacting a bill," he says, and we "cannot simply assume that legislation requires communication."[1]

Greenberg is not alone, of course, in this skepticism about the use of philosophy of language in the legal context, though he is, probably, the most explicit about it. Dworkin has long argued that the content of the law is never determined simply by what lawmakers say; what the law is, is always mediated by some interpretation or other, which, in turn,

[1] See M. Greenberg, "Legislation as Communication? Legal Interpretation and the Study of Linguistic Communication" at 256.

necessarily depends on some moral judgments.[2] Generally speaking, interpretivism in jurisprudence, as this view has come to be called, is rather skeptical of the idea that a better understanding of language and communication helps us to a better understanding of law.

There are many complicated issues involved in this debate. Some of the debate is about the nature of law, and, in particular, about the question of whether law consists of authoritative directives; some of it is about the nature of language; and some of it is about methodological issues concerning the nature of philosophy of law.[3] I cannot hope to address all of these issues here, but I hope to clarify why the commonsense view that the enactment of a law is a speech act, is, indeed, simple common sense and true. This is the task undertaken in the first part of the chapter. In the second part, we will examine the main determinants, semantic and pragmatic, of what the law says.

1. Enactment as a Speech Act

The simple, or "standard" view that I strive to defend here can be stated as follows: the collective action of the legislators enacting a law is a collective speech act, whereby some content is communicated that is, essentially, the content of the law voted on. This communicated content is the legal content of the act. This does not mean, of course, that just about any interpretative question that arises about the content of statutory law is determined by the content communicated by its enactment. Like with any ordinary speech, some content is determined by the content that was successfully communicated by the speaker, and some relevant content might remain undetermined. However, the content that was successfully asserted by the legislature is the legal content of the act; there is no gap between the content asserted by the legislature and the legal content of the act. What the law says is what the law is.[4]

Let us begin with some well-established and not particularly controversial aspects of linguistic communication. People express words

[2] See, for example, R. M. Dworkin, *Law's Empire*, chs. 1–3.

[3] Elsewhere I have dealt in detail with the first and third concerns about interpretivism. See my *Philosophy of Law*, chs. 1–4, and my "Farewell to Conceptual Analysis (in Jurisprudence)."

[4] In chapter 2 we will see that things get more complicated about implicatures and presuppositions.

and sentences in a natural language for a great variety of purposes. There are, as we say, different things one can do in expressing some words (technically called *illocutionary* acts): one can make a statement, that is, convey some propositional content about which we can ask whether it is true or false, but one can also make a promise, ask a question, make a request, issue an invitation, adjourn a meeting, render a verdict, and whatnot. In short, there are numerous kinds of illocutionary acts one can perform by uttering some expression in a natural language, stating or asserting a proposition being only one central case. It is the case, however, in which most philosophers are interested, and for good reason: we normally care about truth, and by and large, only statements expressing some propositional content can be true or false. Consequently, we will also begin by focusing mostly on cases of stating or asserting some propositional content, bearing in mind that it is only one type of illocutionary act that one can perform by a locutionary act (that is, by expressing some words or sentences in a natural language).

It is, of course, an open question whether legal directives are acts of stating or asserting some truth-evaluable content. It is not obvious that legal prescriptions, of the kind we find in statutes or other legal directives, convey any kind of propositional, truth-evaluable content. The view that they do is defended in detail in chapter 3. For now, we will assume that models of an ordinary conversation, whereby speakers state or assert something, provide an adequate theoretical framework that we can use, and deal with modifications and adjustments to legal discourse as we go along.

Another fairly uncontroversial distinction we will use is between different kinds or levels of content that a speaker can convey by expressing something in a given context. Most importantly, it has proved very useful to distinguish between what is *said* or *asserted,* and what is not quite said but *implicated* (or presupposed) by an utterance in a given context of speech. For example, consider a sign at the entrance to an amusement park saying that "Children over age five must purchase a ticket." This sign *says* something about children who are over five years old, that they need to purchase an entrance ticket, but it also *implicates*—though it does not say so—that children under the age of five enter for free. Similarly, if somebody says that "Some of our students failed the qualifying exam," one implicates that some students did not fail the exam, even if this has not been said or asserted. In this chapter, I will focus on what is said, that is, on the *asserted content* of an utterance, and the next chapter is devoted to a detailed discussion of *implicated content*.

Some of what is said or conveyed by any utterance is semantically and syntactically encoded in the words used and the structure of the sentence. We can call this the *semantic content* of an utterance. How much of what is actually conveyed by an utterance in a given context is determined by semantic content is controversial, and some of this controversy will be explored below. There is, however, a wide consensus among philosophers of language and linguists that our ability to comprehend what is said (and implicated) by a linguistic expression is partly enabled and partly constrained by semantics and syntax, but rarely, if ever, quite determined by it. For one thing, we should bear in mind that no sentence or expression has to be used by a speaker according to its ordinary or lexical semantic meaning. And, crucially, even when the speaker utters a sentence that says exactly what it literally or semantically means (and nothing more), the speaker's *intention* to do so is partly what determines what the utterance, on that occasion, states or asserts. In short, expressing an utterance in natural language is, inevitably, a speech act, something one performs with certain intentions.[5] And we normally assume that a speech act succeeds in communicating some content when the speaker's intention to communicate it is fully grasped by the hearer. (More on this below.)

Normally, speech acts, like most other actions, are performed by individuals. Legislation, however, is not an act normally performed by an individual person. It is performed by a group, often consisting of hundreds of people. So the first step in the skeptical journey is to doubt that speech acts (of any kind) can be performed by a group of people, particularly as large and diverse as a legislative assembly. What would be the source of such doubts? Presumably, not the idea that actions are attributable to groups; there are countless examples of intentional actions that we normally and without great difficulty attribute to groups of individuals, as a group. When the USC Trojans play a football game against the UCLA Bruins, the game is played by the two groups, not by individuals, as such; we would say that "the Trojans scored seven points," or that "the Trojans won the game against the Bruins," etc. And these statements are not used figuratively. The group scored the points or won the game, quite literally, even if the

[5] See K. Bach, "Context *ex Machina*" at 27.

actions that count as the actions of the group are performed by individual players, acting in concert with other individual players. Now, of course, playing football is not a speech act. So the question is, is there anything special about *speech* acts that would create a difficulty for the view that groups can perform them?

The ubiquity of the first-person plural in ordinary speech should cast doubt on the idea that people cannot make a collective speech act. *We* can invite you to a party, *we* can make you a promise, *we* can express our condolences, etc. True, in most of these cases, there is an individual speaker who performs the speech act on behalf of the group. Standing next to my wife, I tell you that "We would love to have you over for dinner next week;" I have thus invited you on behalf of myself and my wife. But, of course, my wife and I do not speak in chorus. By using the word "we," I perform the act on behalf of both of us. But now suppose that my wife continues, "How about next Wednesday—would that work for you?" So now it becomes even more clear to you that our invitation is, indeed, a group act, as it were; we both extend it to you, as a couple. Who exactly says what does not really matter, as long as it is clear that the use of the first-person plural was warranted under the circumstances. And, surely, many times it is.

The skeptic might argue that, even if collective speech acts work in some cases, they do not work in the context of a democratic legislative assembly. Individual legislators do not speak on behalf of the legislature, at least not in an orderly democratic regime; they enact laws as a group by voting on bills, not by speaking on behalf of the group as a whole. But, of course, a voting procedure in a legislative institution is precisely the mechanism introduced to enable the collective speech to be performed in an orderly (and presumably democratic) fashion. So the question now is whether voting on a bill is a speech act or not. Greenberg clearly doubts that it is. He points out that different people can vote for something intending to convey very different messages by their votes. By voting for Ralph Nader in the 2000 presidential elections in the U.S., Greenberg reminds us, few voters really intended to convey the message that they wanted Nader to be the president; most of Nader's supporters wanted to convey a very different message, that they were dissatisfied with the traditional two-party system.[6] And, of course, things like that happen all the time.

[6] M. Greenberg, "Legislation as Communication?" at 234.

Different people can say the same thing for different reasons; the fact that people voted for Nader for very different reasons is beside the point. And the fact that many of them intended to convey some additional message, like a symbolic objection to the prevalent political system, is also beside the point. None of this bears on the question of what the content is that is actually asserted by casting a vote in a presidential election. Voting is always an answer to a specific question. The content that is asserted by a vote is the voter's answer to the question. In presidential elections, the question is not: "Who would you really want to become president?" The question is: "How would you like the system to count your vote—in favor of X, Y, or Z?" By voting for X, you convey the message that, in the tally of the votes, your vote counts for X. Now, sure enough, you may have all sorts of reasons for voting for X, and you may want to convey all sorts of additional messages by voting as you did, but it is part of the democratic system of elections that your reasons do not matter. An electoral system does not count reasons; it counts choices. What you say by your vote, the content you assert, as it were, is the choice you have made.

Greenberg is right, of course, that speech acts (like any other action) are often performed with multiple purposes and intentions in mind. But not every kind of intention accompanying a speech act forms part of the content that is asserted by the utterance in question. Consider, for example, a speech act of extending an invitation to a dinner party. Suppose A, B, and C express (separately and unrelatedly) the same invitation to X:

(1) "I would be delighted if you can come to my dinner party next Saturday."

Now suppose that A expressed (1) because A cherishes X's company and would really like him to attend the dinner; B, however, expressed (1) only because X's friends were invited and B did not want to offend X, while C invited X to his dinner only to spite Y, who was not invited. Nevertheless, the utterance expressed by (1) conveys the same assertive content—namely, an invitation to dinner.

None of this is meant to underestimate the complications we may face with electoral systems. Voting is often a very complicated matter, and it might certainly happen that a voting system yields results that are not in line with the actual preferences or intentions of the majority. But these complexities are largely beside the point. The main question here is not whether the voting system guarantees that the preferences of the majority are adequately reflected in the results (in many cases they are not), but whether the act of voting on a proposed bill is a speech act or not. So let us take a simplified model first: suppose that a small committee is assigned the task of suggesting a revision of the undergraduate curriculum of your department. Let us say that there are five committee members and they are expected to come up with a suggestion for a revised curriculum. The committee holds meetings, suggestions are raised and rejected or modified, deliberation goes on for a while, etc. And then, at some point, the committee chair comes up with a suggested revision proposal, which she puts up for a vote. Let us assume that there is a text, written up and available for the committee members to read—call it T—and they are asked whether they approve T or not. So let us assume that four members vote yes and one votes no. Assuming that an ordinary majority is enough here, the result it that T is approved and counts as the recommendation of the committee.

Is there any difficulty with the suggestion that the content of T is the official recommendation of the committee? Presumably not. Then what would count against the suggestion that by voting to approve T, the committee, as a group, *approved* T? Presumably, no difficulties with this formulation either. So what is the difficulty with the suggestion that the committee, as a group, performed a speech act with the intention of communicating the content of T—as a recommended curriculum revision—to the faculty? I fail to see any difficulty with this, either.

Greenberg says, at one point, that "[i]n what is probably the typical case, the legislators have *no* communicative intention associated with the relevant clause of the statutory text. It is uncontroversial that most legislators do not read most of the text of the statutes on which they vote. The vast volume of legislation ensures this."[7] So let us revise our example to accommodate this concern: suppose that one of the committee members who voted for T did not actually read the document; suppose that he only had a very vague and imprecise idea of what the content of T is, yet voted to approve it nevertheless. Even so, it would be very strange if that person also claimed that, though he participated in the vote for T, he did not realize that an affirmative vote counted as a recommendation of the committee, communicated to the faculty

[7] M. Greenberg, "Legislation as Communication?" at 239.

as such. There is little doubt that people who vote for an institutional decision typically know what they are doing; they know that they participate in a decision-making process that results in certain content being communicated as the institutional decision. Perhaps some of the participants in such a process care little, if at all, about what that content is. More often, no doubt, they just rely on others who know better, in effect, delegating their contribution to the collective decision to other members on whom they rely. But I fail to see how any of this makes it doubtful that the collective decision, culminating in the vote on a bill, is a speech act.

Let me generalize the lesson here: voting procedures in a democratic institution are not meant to aggregate the subjective states of mind of the members of the institution. Voting procedures are meant to generate an institutional decision. Participants in such procedures often have many reservations about the resolution they vote for; sometimes they care little about it, or do not even know what exactly they are voting for. In short, voting in a democratic procedure does not necessarily reflect the subjective preferences of the voters. But when legislators vote for approving a certain resolution, they express the intention to communicate the content of the resolution as the official decision of the institution in question. This is what voting on resolutions is, as a matter of social-institutional facts. If you vote in favor of a proposed decision yet fail to realize that you communicate the intention to have the decision approved institutionally, you simply do not know what you are doing. And this does not happen very often, even with legislators.

Those who have doubts that legislation is necessarily a communicative act need only consider the possibility of making law without communicating anything. How would that work? Can we have a legislature (democratic and all) that fails to communicate its laws, keeping them entirely secret? That would not work, presumably. We could not possibly have lawmaking authorities who systematically fail to communicate the laws they make. So I take it that Greenberg's doubts about the "communication model," as he calls it, are not meant to doubt the simple truth that laws cannot be kept secret; they must be conveyed to the public, or at least to some relevant public.

Thus, if there is any plausible worry here, it must lie elsewhere. Now, it is quite true that not every kind of speech act communicates a certain content that is asserted by the speaker. Some speech acts do not assert anything; they do not convey a truth-evaluable content.

A speech act of greeting, for example, communicates something without asserting anything. By saying to an acquaintance, "Good morning," you do not intend to convey the propositional content that the morning is good (or that it ought to be made good, or anything of the sort). You just make a move in a conventional social game, so to speak, conveying your recognition of the convention and compliance with it. The truth-aptness of legislative speech acts, however, is not the point that troubles Greenberg. His argument seems to be that there is no fact of the matter about what counts as the asserted content of legislative speech.

To make this point, Greenberg points out that there is some controversy in the literature in philosophy of language about what exactly constitutes the assertive content of an utterance. According to a Gricean view, the communication intentions of the speaker are entirely constitutive of such content. Whatever the speaker actually intended to say is the content asserted. According to a different view, the subjective intentions of the speaker are only partly constitutive of assertive content; speakers can sometimes fail to communicate all that they had intended to. Therefore, the content that is said or asserted by a speech act partly depends on its reasonable uptake. Assertive content, on this view (that I share), must be defined objectively as the kind of content that a reasonable hearer, with full knowledge of the contextual background of the speech, would understand the speaker to have intended to convey, given what the speaker expressed, the relevant contextual knowledge, and the relevant conversational norms that apply.

But once we introduce some objective element to the definition of assertive content, Greenberg claims, "the particular choice of objective notion will have to be defended on normative grounds.... [O]nce we are not ascertaining the speaker's actual communicative intentions, but imputing communicative content, which content is to be imputed depends in part on what assumptions we make about the speaker."[8]

There are several problems with this argument. To begin with, it is not the case that an objective conception of assertive content has "to be defended on normative grounds"; the objective conception of assertive content points out for us that *there is some normative element* at work here—namely, that what is said by an utterance partly depends on how a reasonable person, knowing all the relevant facts, would understand what the speaker intended to convey. This does not follow from a

[8] M. Greenberg, "Legislation as Communication?" at 232.

normative argument. It follows from the observation that people can fail to convey all that they may have intended to convey. Semantics, for example, is normative through and through, but we do not need a normative argument to establish this fact; it is just a fact about what meaning is, that it consists (at least partly) in following some norms.

It is possible, of course, for legislators, as for any speaker, to intend to assert anything they fancy. A speaker, S, can express the sentence to hearer H, "Please close the door," *intending*, subjectively in his mind, as it were, to convey the request that the hearer shut the window. It is not terribly unusual for people to intend to say something that their hearer cannot possibly infer from the utterance in the context of its expression. According to the traditional Gricean conception, communication intention, like any other intention, is a purely subjective notion, a fact about the mental state of the speaker. And that seems quite right, but it does not necessarily settle what assertive content is. We have two kinds of facts here: 1) facts about the intentions of speakers, the communication intentions, pertaining to what they intended to say by uttering T to H in circumstances C; and 2) objective facts, facts about what a reasonable hearer, sharing all of the relevant epistemic background in C, would infer that S had intended to convey by uttering T in C. And these two facts may come apart. So which one can we properly call *the assertive content of the utterance*: the one subjectively intended by the speaker or the one that consists in reasonable uptake?

One way to make sense of Greenberg's concern here is to think that the answer depends on the hearer's interest in the utterance in question and her reasons for paying attention to it. And that may give some plausibility to the idea that the choice between the subjective notion of assertive content and the objective notion of it is a normative one, presumably depending on considerations about which type of content we should care about in particular conversational contexts. Now, it is certainly true that our interests in different kinds of assertions may direct us to closer or lesser attention to the subjective intentions of speakers. In intimate conversations, we care more about intentions than about what is said, in some objective sense of it; and, of course, in law, it is arguable that judges should care about what the law actually says, not about what the lawmakers may have intended to say.[9] But this is, indeed, a normative issue, one that pertains to the question of what reasons we have to pay attention to various aspects of linguistic

[9] More on this point in chapter 5.

communication. A psychologist may care more about *why* you say something, perhaps in a subconscious sense, than about the content of what you say, because that is her job. But it does not mean that the assertive content of your expressions in a session with a psychologist is determined by your motives, hidden or not, for saying what you say. It only means that the psychologist has reasons to pay attention to something else, not only, or perhaps even primarily, to what your expressions actually assert. Similarly, sometimes we have reasons to pay attention to what the speaker intended to convey, even if she failed to convey it. This would not render assertive content subjective; it simply means that assertive content is not the only thing hearers might be interested in. And this, of course, might be true about legislation as well. In various contexts of statutory interpretation, and for various purposes, we may care about other communicative aspects of a legislative speech act besides what it says.

Stephen Neale, however, insists that all we have here are two kinds of facts—facts about intentions and facts about reasonable uptake—and none of these types of facts can be privileged to capture some pre-theoretical notion of "assertive content."[10] I am not sure that this is quite right. In fact, it may be the other way around: pre-theoretically there is a very clear distinction between what a speaker actually said and what she may have intended to say. Normally, we do not get confused about this. If my wife asks me to close the door, but I happen to know that she misspoke and what she really intended to request was to have me shut the window, I would go and shut the window. But it would be very odd to suggest that what my wife actually *said* is "Shut the window," even if the utterance she expressed is "Close the door." We would rather want to say that she intended to ask me to shut the window though what she actually asserted was a request to close the door. So there is some intuitive, pre-theoretical notion of asserted content that is objective, as opposed to the subjective notion of what a speaker intended to say, just as there is a pre-theoretical notion of a distinction between intending or trying to do something and doing it; people do not always do what they try or intend to do. I may intend to open the door by pushing it outward, but if the door opens inward, I am actually shutting the door (or keeping it shut, as the case may be), not opening

[10] See his "Textualism with Intent." The specific point I attribute to Neale in the text comes from a public exchange during a conference presentation at Fordham Law School on constitutional interpretation, held in March 2013.

it. Theoretically speaking, we must make room for the possibility that a speaker can fail to express what she may have wanted to express; what an utterance in a given context actually says might not be what the speaker intended to say. So there are some good reasons, intuitive and theoretical, to understand the notion of asserted content objectively, as the kind of content that a reasonable hearer, sharing the relevant contextual knowledge, would infer that the utterance says in the context of its expression.

To conclude, Greenberg's doubts about the legislative procedure as a form of collective speech act stem from a confusion between the question of what kind of communicative action legislation is and the very different question of whether voting, or legislation more generally, necessarily reflects the subjective intentions of the legislators. The fact that the answer to the second question is often *no* does not cast any doubt on the assumption that voting in a democratic legislature to approve a certain bill is a form of collective speech act intending to communicate the content of the bill as the official, institutional decision of the legislature.

Let me acknowledge, however, the incompleteness of the argument here. I have said nothing to support the underlying assumption that a legislature's authoritative directive is the law. In other words, I have only shown that a legislative-institutional decision, in the form of enacting a law, is a speech act that communicates the law intended to be enacted. More needs to be said, of course, to substantiate the claim that the law just is whatever legal authorities communicate as legal directives. Such an argument would pertain to the fundamental nature of law and its essential authoritative nature. This is not an argument I will undertake to defend here; I have done that elsewhere.[11]

2. Pragmatic Enrichment

Let us now take a closer look at the relations between semantic determinants of what is said or asserted, and contextual or, more generally, pragmatic determinants. We defined the notion of *semantic content* as the kind of content that is fully determined by semantics and syntax, that is, by the lexical meaning of the words used and the syntax of the

[11] See, for example, my *Philosophy of Law*, chs. 3–4.

sentence. Note that it is a fairly narrow understanding of "semantics" that I assume here, and advisedly so. Namely, I assume (following Bach, Salmon, Soames, and others) that semantic properties are properties of words and sentences, not of utterances or speech acts.[12] This allows us to characterize the semantic features of a natural language as those that are basically rule or norm governed, public, and learnable—the aspects of a natural language that one needs to acquire in order to be able to engage in linguistic communication.[13] Semantic meaning (and syntax) is the main vehicle we use to convey content by linguistic communication, and we can use it as a vehicle precisely because it is rule governed, public, and learnable. Furthermore, we should never lose sight of the most remarkable feature of the combination of semantic and syntactical features of sentences in a natural language, perhaps the most remarkable achievement of our species, which is the ability to compose an infinite number of different, meaningful sentences with a finite set of words and syntactical rules, called "compositionality." It would be very difficult, not say impossible, to account for the compositionality of natural language if we did not take seriously the idea that words are signs, or as Salmon calls them, "expression-types," and not expression tokens, and signs signify—symbolize or represent, that is—in a public and learnable manner. And "[t]his systematic assignment of representation is semantics," as Salmon puts it.[14] The question of just how much communicated content is actually determined by semantically encoded representation is something that I will get back to shortly. For now, we just need the idea that some content is semantically encoded in expressions using natural language.

The *assertive content* of an utterance, what the speaker *says* on an occasion of speech, is the truth-evaluable content that the utterance conveys on that occasion. It is the complete proposition asserted by the speaker about which we can ask whether it is true or false.[15] In the last few decades, there has been a growing awareness among philosophers

[12] The speech-act conception of semantics is probably a legacy of Wittgenstein's later philosophy.

[13] Needless to say, I am taking no position here about the question of whether any deep aspects of syntax of natural languages are innate knowledge, as Chomsky famously argued. Even if they are, surface grammar needs to be learned or acquired, and certainly meaning of words is learnable.

[14] N. Salmon, "Two Conceptions of Semantics" at 323.

[15] Assuming, of course, that it is the kind of utterance which purports to have some propositional content. As mentioned earlier, not all expressions are truth-apt. More on this in chapter 3.

of language and linguists that the assertive content of an utterance, what the speaker says on an occasion of speech, is often, perhaps even most often in ordinary conversations, under-determined by the semantic content of the expression uttered. In many, if not most, cases or ordinary utterances, the assertive content is the *pragmatically enriched* content that the speaker intended to convey, and the hearer can recognize it as such. Thus, when a hearer grasps the assertive content of an utterance, it is normally a defeasible *inference* drawn by the hearer from the meaning of the sentence uttered (semantics and syntax), some contextual knowledge of the relevant speech situation, and, as we will discuss in detail in the next chapter, some normative framework governing the conversation. To see why contextual knowledge often plays a crucial role in the inference of what is said, it might be best to demonstrate with some familiar examples.

Consider, first, expressions using pure indexicals, such as "I," "today," "now," "here," etc. Obviously, in such cases, what is said is partly determined by objective features of the speech situation, such as who is the speaker, what is the present time and place, etc. Admittedly, some philosophers do not see pure indexicals as examples of a gap between sematic and assertive content because there is a widely shared view that the meaning of pure indexicals just is their reference on any particular occasion of use.[16] According to this view, an expression of the kind, "I am walking right now," semantically determines all of the content that is conveyed (assuming that the sentence is not expressed ironically, figuratively, or such), even if, obviously, the content depends on some objective features of the speech situation. Perhaps, but then, of course, other types of cases abound. Demonstratives, such as "they," "she," "that," etc., behave differently because it is not plausible to assume that demonstratives simply mean what they refer to in a given expression. When a speaker says, "She went to get some coffee," the speaker must assume that the hearer is able to recognize the reference of "she," that there is some salient feature of the contextual background, shared by speaker and hearer, that enables parties to the conversation to pick out or recognize the person "she" refers to. Normally, this would follow from previous stages of the conversation.

Not surprisingly, the use of indexicals and demonstratives in statutory language is almost nonexistent. Precisely because it is rather

[16] D. Kaplan, "Demonstratives: An essay on the Semantics, Logic, Metaphysics and Epistemology of Demonstratives and Other Indexicals."

obvious that the use of such terms renders the communicated content very context-dependent, legal formulations would normally try to avoid them. If the law needs to set a deadline, for example, it would mention a specific date, not use such expressions as "next week."

In any case, we have many other examples, besides demonstratives, where semantic meaning under-determines what the speaker says. Consider the cases below, which are not meant to be exhaustive, of course:

a. *Incomplete propositions*
   "I have had enough" [of what?], "It's raining" [where, when?], "Tom is too short" [for what?]
b. *Possessive ascriptions*
   "Joseph's book..." [the book that belongs to Joseph, written by Joseph, in Joseph's hands, etc.]
c. *Numerical phrases*
   "You have two hours to take the exam" [at most two]
   "I have two daughters" [two and only two]
   "Anyone with two children is eligible for a child-support tax credit" [at least two]
d. *Domain quantifiers*
   "*Everyone* must stop writing [the exam] now" [everyone in the classroom, not everyone in the world]
e. *Time/causal sequence*
   "Sarah ate her breakfast *and* went to work" [first ate breakfast, then went to work]
   "John fell asleep while driving *and* his car swerved off the road" [causal relation]
f. *Contextual anaphora*
   "I have nothing to wear" [for the occasion, and not: "I have no clothes in my possession"]
   "Don't worry, you are not going to die" [from this injury, and not: "You are never going to die"]
   "John and Susan went to Paris last summer" [together]
   "I haven't had any breakfast" [yet today]

Obviously, context plays a crucial role in the hearer's ability to infer the complete propositional content asserted in these and countless similar examples. Let me adopt the phrase suggested by John Perry and call the pragmatic determinants that bear on the inference of assertive content "near-side pragmatics," as opposed to those that bear on implicated content, which will be labeled "far-side pragmatics."[17] Either way, context is meant here as an *epistemic* notion. The pragmatically relevant context of an utterance consists of the elements that the speaker assumes to be known (or taken for granted[18]) by the hearer and known by the hearer to be assumed by the speaker. For some purposes it will turn out to be useful to distinguish between context as general background knowledge, consisting of the kind of knowledge that ordinary people share about the world, and context that is specific to the particular speech situation in question. Quite clearly, for example, the kind of contextual knowledge that is essential for grasping the propositional content in cases of *incomplete propositions* (and, typically, *possessive ascriptions*) is fairly specific to the particular speech situation. But in other cases, such as *time/causal sequence* and *domain quantifiers*, general background knowledge is typically quite sufficient. The same goes for the examples of *contextual anaphora* (we just know that generally people have some clothes, that everybody dies at some point, or that hardly anyone has not had breakfast in their lives).

Nothing is uncontroversial in philosophy, however, and there are two skeptical positions about the picture that I am assuming here. To recap, the picture is this: in cases of an ordinary conversation, particularly when the utterance is a statement of some sort, what is said by the speaker is very often, but not always and not necessarily, pragmatically enriched content. Now, on the one hand, some philosophers (Stanley and King[19]) have raised doubts about near-side pragmatics and how much of a role context really plays in determining what is said. On the other side, contextualist semanticists (Recanati, for example[20]) doubt that pragmatic enrichment is an exception in any way, arguing that semantically encoded content always varies with

[17] I am assuming here that there is no substantive difference between near-side and far-side pragmatics; the difference is only in what pragmatic factors determine: whether they determine the asserted content or content that is not quite asserted but somehow implicated.

[18] As we will see in the next chapter, speakers sometimes take for granted that the hearer would be willing to accommodate some background information that is relevant to their utterance. Soames calls this "presupposition accommodation."

[19] J. King and J. Stanley, "Semantics, Pragmatics, and the Role of Semantic Content," cf. R. A. Carston, "Explicature and Semantics," and S. Soames, "Drawing the Line between Meaning and Implicature—and Relating Both to Assertion," in *Philosophical Essays, Vol. 1.*

[20] F. Recanati, "Contextualism and Anti-Contextualism in the Philosophy of Language." A similar view, called *dynamic semantics*, has gained some support amongst linguists recently.

context; the kind of content that is encoded by semantic features of words and sentences is totally in flux, varying with context of utterance on each particular occasion.

I want to hold on to the middle ground. The skepticism about near-side pragmatics seems to me theoretically under-motivated. In order to give some plausible account for the obvious examples of near-side pragmatic enrichment, of the kind we mentioned above, the skeptics need to argue that either pragmatically enriched content is at least semantically triggered, if not entirely encoded or, in other cases, where no such sematic trigger is in sight, the enriched content is only implicated but not quite asserted. Let us focus on the latter. It is not entirely implausible to argue that, in some of these examples, in particular, *time/causal sequence* and *contextual anaphora*, the enriched content is not quite said but only implicated. Perhaps these are borderline cases. But then it becomes a bit mysterious why we should insist on a sharp demarcation line between near-side and far-side pragmatics. The skeptics do not deny that far-side pragmatics is genuine; they do not wish to doubt that pragmatic determinants are essential for the inference of implicated content. But if the distinction between what is said and what is implicated is a bit blurred sometimes—as the skeptics must maintain in order to account for the examples—then the motivation for denying pragmatic enrichment about what is said, while allowing it for what is implicated, becomes theoretically under-motivated.[21]

The radical contextualist view, on the other hand, is really about semantics, not about pragmatic enrichment. It is a view about what meaning is, in the pure semantic sense. Needless to say, this is not the place to venture into complex issues in semantics. But the doubts I will raise about near-side pragmatics in the legal context should make contextualism take some pause. As we will see in the next section, legislatures manage to say most of what they want to say with very minimal contextual presuppositions and very limited pragmatic enrichment. None of this should mean, of course, that law can prove contextualism wrong. But it can prove, or at least I will try to prove, that semantically encoded information plays a much greater role in law than in ordinary conversational contexts.

[21] None of this is meant to deny that there are many cases in which the implicated content is semantically triggered and, sometimes, semantically encoded. I will discuss these categories, which are quite important to law, in the next chapter.

3. Near-Side Pragmatics in Law

The role of near-side pragmatics in law is much more limited than in ordinary conversations, for two main reasons. First, legal directives are not casual statements uttered in an ordinary conversation. Legislatures do not tend to enact half-baked formulations and incomplete sentences. Laws are usually crafted carefully and formulated with the intention of addressing a wide and diverse audience. Second, we must bear in mind that the contextual background of legislation is relatively opaque, often rather complex, and less known to the hearers than in cases of ordinary conversation.

Consider, for example, Lon Fuller's famous hypothetical of a city ordinance saying that "it is a misdemeanor to sleep in any railway station,"[22] and assume that an elderly gentleman, sitting on the bench waiting for his train late at night, dozes off for a few minutes. Surely we would not want to conclude that this elderly gentleman violated the ordinance. Can we say that, although the law is expressed in terms of "*to sleep in* [a] railway station," what the ordinance actually asserts is something else, more like "to use the railway station as a place to sleep in"? This is something that our gentleman clearly did not attempt to do. In other words, the suggestion here is that the contextually enriched content asserted by this ordinance is somewhat different from its semantic content; what the law says is not exactly what the words mean. In considering this option, Scott Soames remarked that this analysis might be a stretch: "Although one can imagine completions of the story in which the lawmakers really did understand themselves to be so asserting the contextually enriched context that gives the desired results, one can also imagine completions in which they did not give the matter much thought."[23]

The point of Soames's remark here, I take it, is that contextual knowledge in the legislative context is often very limited and partial, and therefore pragmatic enrichment is often more in doubt than we would otherwise encounter in ordinary conversations. Perhaps the city ordinance is poorly drafted, but that does not mean that a sensible reading of it is what the ordinance actually asserts. The legislature is a complex institution, and, in some cases, there is just no answer to the question of what exactly the legislature said.

[22] L. Fuller, "Positivism and Fidelity to Law: A Reply to Professor Hart," *71 Harvard Law Rev* (1958), 630.

[23] S. Soames, "Interpreting Legal Texts: What Is and What Is Not Special about the Law," in *Philosophical Essays, Vol. 1*.

A famous case in point is *Holy Trinity v. U.S.*, from 1892.[24] The relevant congressional act prescribed that it is forbidden to facilitate the immigration of laborers to the country. The purpose of this law was to try to reduce the influx of cheap unskilled labor, which, at the time, was seen as a major draw on the U.S. labor market. However, the relevant part of the law was phrased as forbidding the importation of "labor or service of any kind." In this case, a high-ranking clergyman was brought from England to serve as the rector of the Holy Trinity Church in New York, and the question was whether the act really forbids importation of this kind of labor, or whether it is confined to manual labor.[25] The court held that the use of the word "labor" in this act is, indeed, confined to manual labor and does not apply to clergymen. The specific grounds for this decision (some of which were rather obscure) should not detain us here. The question is whether it would make sense to suggest that the court simply identified the pragmatically enriched *assertive content* of the congressional speech.

Critics of this decision pointed to the legislative history of this act, and they have shown that it is rather convoluted and murky. We know that there was some discussion in the earlier stages of the congressional debate about this specific question. Some congressmen suggested using the expression "manual labor" in the act. Others thought that it would be redundant, while others expressed the hope that the language would be clarified in subsequent amendment to the act (as it was, actually). However, when the act was voted on during the next congressional session, the issue did not come up again, partly because of time constraints and the fear of some of the leaders in Congress that the momentum for the legislation might be lost if it were to get bogged down in too many details. The reason for this murkiness is not difficult to surmise. It is pretty clear from the context of the legislation that its purpose was to stop the influx of cheap unskilled labor. But it is equally clear that Congress must have felt uncomfortable in making this focus on manual labor all too explicit. It must have been politically rather inconvenient to explicitly declare that the law targets the importation of cheap manual labor.[26]

[24] *Rector, Holy Trinity Church v. United States*, 143 U.S. 457 (1892).

[25] A separate section in the statute contained a list of explicit exceptions to the prohibition, but none of them applied to clergymen. More on this in chapter 2.

[26] For the legislative history of *Holy Trinity*, see for example C. Chomsky in Eskridge, Frickey and Garrett, eds., *Statutory Interpretation Stories* at 15–26.

The legislative history of *Holy Trinity*, which is not all that unique, of course, is a cautionary tale. It reminds us that the context of legal speech can be rather murky. Remember that the concept of context here is to be understood epistemically; assertive content is enriched by contextual factors that are common knowledge between speaker and hearer. Only factors that parties to the conversation are aware of or take for granted can contribute to the inference of pragmatically enriched content. When crucial contextual factors are unknown to the hearers, and speakers can be assumed to know that, then inference to enriched content becomes doubtful as well. Furthermore, we need to bear in mind that the hearers, in the legal case, are not really parties to the conversation that generates statutory law. Judges and administrative agencies, entrusted with the application of the law to concrete instances, are remote conversants, with rather limited access to the specific context in which the relevant piece of legislation is enacted.

At this point, however, it might be useful to recall the distinction between contextual knowledge that is specific to the particular conversation, and general background knowledge speakers and hearers widely share. The particular complexity and relative opaqueness of legislative processes certainly bears on the kind of specific contextual knowledge that constitutes the pragmatic determinants of legislative speech. But general background knowledge is not necessarily affected by any of this. Therefore, there is nothing to rule out the possibility that the assertive content of statutory law is pragmatically enriched by some general, background, contextual knowledge. A simple example is disambiguation of lexically ambiguous terms: a legal directive regulating the opening hours of "banks" asserts something about commercial institutions, not river banks, and we knows this simply by knowing some general facts about the world surrounding us (viz., that commercial institutions have opening hours and rivers do not). Disambiguation is not the only example, however. In New York City, one can observe signs posted on doors in public buildings, pursuant to the NYC Administrative Code Title 27, Article 371, Paragraph C, saying that the "Doors must remain closed at all times." Surely we would not think that the directive instructed us never to open the door, only to make sure that we close it after use. And again, we infer this content because we know that a door that must remain closed at all times—literally at all times, that is—means that it cannot be used as a door anymore. Similarly, a traffic regulation requiring drivers to keep their eyes on the road at all times would not be violated by the natural blinking of the eyes.

Between the contextual background that is relatively specific to the particular conversation in question—which is problematic in legislative context—and general background knowledge shared by ordinary people at the relevant time—which is not so problematic—an interesting intermediary case in the legal context gives rise to many controversies in statutory interpretation, namely, the background that pertains to the reasons that give rise to the particular legislative act. Laws are enacted for reasons, with some purposes in mind as to what the law is meant to achieve, the normative changes it purports to introduce, and the reasons for those intended changes. We can simply call all this the *legislative purpose*. As we will see later, in chapter 4, legislative purpose is particularly important in guiding the courts' role in the precisification of vague terms applied to borderline cases. I doubt, however, that legislative purpose is playing much of a role in the pragmatic enrichment of *asserted content* of legislation. Consider, once again, the Fuller hypothetical about the municipal ordinance prohibiting people from sleeping in railway stations: assuming that the purpose of this law is to keep homeless people from turning railway stations into their nighttime lodging places, it would be very sensible to infer that what the ordinance actually *asserts* is that it is forbidden "to use the railway station as a place to sleep in." No doubt, this would be a sensible reading of the ordinance in light of the above-mentioned purpose. But is the inference secure enough here?

Two considerations count against it. First, the knowledge we have about legislative purposes is often limited and, more importantly, often partial and incomplete. In most cases, we know what prompts the legislature to act; we know the background social, political, or economic problems that initially motivate a piece of legislation. However, legislatures often use a particular social problem to motivate an act, while trying to solve other problems in its vicinity as well. In other words, legislative purposes are not necessarily exhausted by the particular "mischief" that motivates them to enact a new law. Often other, related purposes pile on in the process of the enactment, and outsiders may have limited knowledge of those additional purposes. Or, as sometimes happens, those additional purposes may be very controversial, even among legislators who voted for the bill in question.

Second, and more importantly, even if we are fully aware of the legislative purposes in play, there is no guarantee that the formulation of the law effectively expresses those purposes. In other words, legislatures do not always succeed in saying what they should have said in light of their purposes or the objectives they intend to achieve. If the purpose of the municipal ordinance was to keep railway stations from becoming lodging places for homeless people, it should have said that it is forbidden "to use the railway station as a place to sleep in," but that is not what the law says. What it says is that it is forbidden "to sleep" in the station. The move from the reasons for saying something and what is actually said is a matter of fact, not a logical inference; speakers, including legislatures, of course, can fail to actually say what they really should have said given their purposes or aims in the conversation.

A famous example is the case of *Whiteley v. Chappell*. The relevant statute made it an offense to fraudulently "personate any person entitled to vote."[27] The defendant had fraudulently voted in the name of his neighbor, whose name was on the voter rolls, but who also happened to be dead by then. There is little doubt that the purpose of the law was to make it an offense to vote fraudulently by impersonating anyone else, and the defendant's conduct is precisely the kind that should have been covered by the definition of this offense. Alas, the law was badly formulated, making it an offense to impersonate only those who are "entitled to vote." Dead people do not fall into this category. The court therefore concluded that the defendant's conduct did not fall within the bounds of the criminal offense. From a linguistic perspective, this was the right decision. Whether the court should have chosen to ignore what the law says in favor of a more purposive interpretation is a separate, normative question, which I do not purport to answer here.

To be sure, I would not rule out the possibility that the known purpose of a given piece of legislation contributes to the pragmatically enriched content of what it actually says. But I doubt that this is a frequent phenomenon. Once again, none of this is meant to suggest that judges should ignore legislative purposes when interpretation of a statutory law is called for. Nor does it entail that, when the law says something that is at odds with the clear and undeniable purpose of the law, judges should implement what the law says and not what the law should have said under the circumstances. Judges may well have

[27] (1868) L.R. 4 Q.B. 147, 147.

a moral obligation to ignore what the law says when not doing so would result in very bad consequences. These are normative questions, and, as such, they are certainly not determined by the kind of linguistic considerations we are exploring here.

The conclusion that emerges so far is not trivial: our discussion aimed to show that, in the context of statutory law, the gap between semantic and assertive content is much more limited and infrequent compared with ordinary conversations. In ordinary conversations, the content that is actually asserted by a speaker is very frequently pragmatically enriched content. Pragmatic enrichment is not so prevalent in the legislative context. Legislatures are aware of the fact that they need to convey the legal content that they want to convey to a large and diverse audience, they know that the exact formulation of the law will be subject to close scrutiny by lawyers and the courts, and they know that the conversational context of the legislation is relatively opaque. Therefore, it should come as no surprise that what the law says is, much more frequently than not, exactly what the words and sentences used literally mean, while sometimes, of course, using technical language and doctrinal understandings of terms that lawyers widely share.

The conclusion that there is rarely a gap between the semantic and the assertive content of statutory law is also supported by the procedural aspects of legislation in democratic assemblies. Laws are drafted, carefully or not, as the case may be, but then they tend to be revised, redrafted, negotiated on, etc., until some final text emerges that is put for an up-or-down vote. The law, of course, is the final text that is voted on. Therefore, when legislators vote on a proposed bill, their communication intention, individually and collectively, if you will, is to vote for (or against) whatever it is that the proposed bill, the final text, means in the context of its enactment; voting for a bill is the communication intention to convey the assertive/legal content that is encoded in the text that is put to the final vote. Now, of course, it is possible that what the text says, its assertive content, is not exactly what the words and sentences literally mean. Legislators intend to vote for what the bill says, not for a dictionary rendition of words on paper. However, given the collective and rather complex nature of this procedure, there is not much room for a gap between what the legislative text would literally mean and what it asserts in the context of its enactment. Normally, what the law asserts just is the public-sematic meaning of the text voted upon. In other words, voting procedures make it the case that, in all but very unusual circumstances, the communication intention of the legislators is, almost inevitably, the intention to assert what the text of the bill publicly means—that is, to assert the semantic content of the bill in question.

Once again, let me emphasize that I am not denying the possibility of pragmatic enrichment of assertive content in statutory law. It certainly happens that the assertive content of a piece of legislation is somewhat different from the semantic meaning of the expression used, particularly when the pragmatic determinants in play are a matter of general knowledge. My doubts pertain to the relative frequency of this phenomenon. In ordinary conversations, pragmatic enrichment is the norm, not the exception; in statutory law, it is the exception.

2

What Does the Law Implicate?

In countless instances of ordinary speech, some communicative content is implicated, though not quite asserted, by the speaker in the particular context of his utterance. It is, therefore, natural to assume that legislative speech would also contain a great deal of content that is implicated by what the law says. For reasons that will be explained in chapter 5, textualists are particularly drawn to the idea that much can be inferred about the content of statutory law by paying attention to what legal language implicates. Examples are not difficult to come by: if a statutory provision lists a number of well-defined exceptions to a norm, it would seem to implicate that no other exceptions should be allowed; if the law says that "All Xs who are F ought to φ," it would seem to implicate that there must be Xs who are not F, and they need not φ. Or, to take a more concrete example, consider a municipal ordinance requiring restaurants "to have clean and well-maintained bathrooms indoors." Even if the regulation does not explicitly say so, surely we would assume that a restaurant that had impeccable bathrooms that are kept locked at all times would violate the ordinance. That the restrooms need to be open for patrons to use is content that is clearly implicated by such an ordinance.

The purpose of this chapter is to present the main forms in which a certain communicative content may be implicated by an utterance, and explore the ways in which such implications might work in the legal context. My main argument is going to be that the strategic nature of legal discourse casts some doubt about the reliability of implicated content in statutory law. I will try to show that both legislatures and courts have an interest in maintaining a certain level of uncertainty about the normative framework of the discourse, in ways that allow both parties to manipulate content that has only been implicated, but not actually asserted, by the law.

1. Varieties of Implication

Generally, the implied content of the utterance of P in context C can be defined as the content that the speaker, in the specific context of C, is *committed to* by uttering P, and the hearers are expected to know that the speaker is committed to, and the speaker can be expected to know this. A speaker can be expected to be committed to a certain implied content if and only if an explicit, ex post denial of the implied content would strike any *reasonable* hearer under the circumstances as perplexing, disingenuous, or contradictory. There are several kinds of implied content. The two most familiar cases are implicatures and utterance presuppositions, and these are the cases that I will discuss here.[1]

a. Conversational implicatures

Let us begin with a very brief review of some of Grice's main ideas about implicatures.[2] His main insight is that our ability to understand content of expressions beyond what is said[3] is due to a combination of two kinds of factors: general norms of conversation that apply to the relevant speech situation, and contextual knowledge that is shared by speaker and hearer in the circumstances of the utterance. Implicatures are, of course, pragmatically enriched content, and, as such, they are derived by a defeasible inference from semantic content, contextual knowledge, and, crucially, some normative framework that applies to the conversation in question. In normal conversational situations, when the main purpose of speech is the cooperative exchange of information, certain general maxims apply. Grice helpfully listed and

[1] Irony is another example, but I will not discuss it here. Irony is a rather special case, typically implicating that the speaker intends to convey the opposite of the assertive content of his utterance. Some forms of metaphor may also implicate content beyond what is said, and there may be other cases.

[2] P. Grice, *Studies in the Way of Words* at 24–37.

[3] There is some uncertainty about Grice's own views concerning the role of near-side pragmatics. At many points Grice talks about pragmatic enrichment as content that goes beyond what *is said*; it is not entirely clear that Grice was aware of the ubiquity of pragmatically enriched assertive content. See S. Soames, "Drawing the Line between Meaning and Implicature," in *Philosophical Essays, Vol. 1*.

classified these maxims of ordinary conversation, and they are basically as follows:

(i) *maxim of quantity*—make your conversational contribution as informative as required, viz., do not say too little and do not say too much;
(ii) *maxims of quality*—do not say what you believe to be false, and do not say something if you do not have adequate evidence for it;
(iii) *maxim of relevance*—make your contribution relevant to the conversation;
(iv) *maxims of manner*—avoid obscurity and ambiguity; be brief and orderly.[4]

As noted, these maxims apply to ordinary conversations where the purpose of the conversation is the cooperative exchange of information. The maxims are norms that directly instantiate the specific functions or purposes of communicative interactions and facilitate those cooperative functions. In fact, the maxims are normative in two standard senses of normativity: they are norms in the social sense—namely, in that they are generally followed in ordinary conversations—and they are norms in the robust or philosophical sense of normativity, namely, in being supported by reasons that make them the kind of norms that ought to be followed, given the cooperative purpose of the conversation.[5] Over the years, some philosophers and linguists have suggested reformulations of these maxims, aiming to come up with more economical formulations, subsuming various Gricean maxims under more general heuristics. Without attempting to imply that these formulations make no progress, I will largely adhere to Grice's original maxims, mostly because the reformulations make no difference to the arguments deployed in this chapter. Perhaps the maxims that Grice listed can be streamlined and subsumed under fewer heuristics; I remain agnostic about this.[6]

[4] Grice, *Studies in the Way of Words* at 28.

[5] See Grice, *Studies in the Way of Words* at 29, acknowledging this duality very explicitly.

[6] Some of the neo-Gricean heuristics that have been suggested in the literature remain faithful to the idea that the maxims are norms. Others, however, have shifted the focus to cognitive principles that purport to describe how our mind actually works in working out communicative content from utterances. Most influential in this line of work is, of course, the relevance theory developed by D. Sperber and D. Wilson, *Relevance: Communication and Cognition*. I do not think that there is a necessary contradiction or tension between these two general outlooks on pragmatics; most often they work nicely together. But they are different outlooks, aiming to explain somewhat different things. None of what I argue in this, and other chapters, will concern relevance theories.

Be this as it may, a certain content is conversationally implicated by a speaker if it is not part of what the speaker had actually asserted, but nevertheless is implicated by what he said in the specific speech situation, given the conversational maxims that apply. In other words, a speaker S conversationally implicates q by saying p in context C, if:

(i) S is presumed to observe the relevant conversational maxims in C;
(ii) the assumption that S meant (or intended that) q is required to make sense of S's utterance of p in context C, given the conversational maxims that apply;
(iii) S believes/assumes that his/her hearers can recognize condition (ii), and can recognize that S knows that.[7]

As Grice himself emphasized, two main features are essentially associated with conversational implicatures:

(i) Conversational implicatures are always *cancelable* by the speaker. The speaker can always add an explicit clarification to cancel the implication that would otherwise follow from his utterance. As we shall see, this is an essential feature of conversational implicatures.
(ii) Conversational implicatures are results of a *defeasible inference* by the hearer; there is always some derivation, as Grice called it, which leads the hearer to construe the content of an implicature.

The second condition needs to be qualified, however. In addition to regular conversational implicatures, Grice also identified a category of cases he called *generalized conversational implicatures*. His examples are the following:

> Anyone who uses a sentence of the form X *is meeting a woman this evening* would normally implicate that the person to be met was someone other than X's wife, mother, sister or perhaps even close Platonic friend. Similarly, if I were to say X *went into a house yesterday and found a tortoise inside the front door*, my hearer would normally be surprised if some time later I revealed the house was X's own.[8]

Generalized conversational implicatures are those in which an expression is used that would normally implicate a certain content, unless

[7] Note that the last condition, of transparency, is actually rather problematic and controversial. Grice himself was aware of a serious problem here considering the implicatures involved in using disjunction. See, for example, S. Soames, "Drawing the Line between Meaning and Implicature," in *Philosophical Essays, Vol. 1*.

[8] Grice, *Studies in the Way of Words* at 37.

that implication is explicitly canceled. A speaker can say, "X is meeting a woman this evening," and immediately add, "I wonder whether the woman is X's wife or not." Here, the implicature is explicitly canceled by the latter sentence. Now, what Grice seems to suggest is that, in the non-canceled cases, when somebody says "an A," the expression would normally implicate that one has no specific knowledge about it or that one deems it irrelevant to the conversation to specify whose A it is. Otherwise the speaker would fail to follow the conversational maxim of quantity (do not say too little).[9] In other words, generalized conversational implicatures are created by a combination of the semantic features of certain standard expressions in natural language; they are semantically triggered, hence the generality, and particular contexts in which the conversational maxims apply. Expressions of the form "an A" are semantically such that they trigger a certain type of expectation; given the conversational maxims that apply in concrete speech situations, this expectation normally generates an implicature.

Cases of generalized conversational implicatures should be distinguished, however, from another familiar type of case, in which a certain implicature has been used so frequently that it has actually become an idiomatic expression, with a conventional meaning that differs, somewhat, from the literal meaning of the words used. Examples are very familiar: "Do you have the time?"—which is not normally used as a question about possession but to ask the hearer what time it is. Similarly, "Can you pass me the salt?" is typically used to make a request, not to ask the hearer about his or her ability to do something. These expressions have long gained a certain conventional meaning, which is no longer a matter of implicature.[10]

b. *Presuppositions*

In addition to content that is conversationally implicated by an utterance in a given context, there are many cases in which a given utterance would only make sense if a certain content is presupposed by the speaker in relation to the background knowledge shared by his

[9] In some cases it might seem that "an X" would carry more specific information. Compare "I found an earring" with "I lost an earring"—clearly in the latter case, the implication is that the earring was mine. But I think this follows from the meaning of "lost"; I can lose only that which had been in my possession at some earlier time.

[10] See, for example, K. Bach and R. M. Harnish, *Communication and Speech Acts* at 173. Searle refers to these cases as conventionally used indirect speech acts, *Expression and Meaning* at 36–43.

hearers. A presupposition consists in content that is not asserted, but would need to be taken for granted to make sense of the asserted content or its relevance to the conversation. This is the type of content that is either already shared by the conversational participants, or that the hearers would be willing to accommodate for the purpose of the conversation. The interesting cases, however, are those in which we can infer the presupposition from the utterance itself. Soames defines *utterance presuppositions* as follows:

> An utterance U presupposes P if one can reasonably infer from U that the speaker S accepts P and regards it as uncontroversial, either because:
>
> (a) S thinks that P is already part of the conversational background at the time of U; or because
>
> (b) S thinks that the conversational participants are prepared to add P, without objection, to the background.[11]

Consider the following examples:

(1) "Bill regrets lying to his parents."
Presupposition: Bill [believes that he] lied to his parents.[12]

(2) "Sarah forgot to pick up Jane from the airport."
Presupposition: Sarah was supposed (or intended) to pick Jane up at the airport.

(3) "John's wife is going to the concert tomorrow."
Presupposition: John is married.

Some linguists have noted that a speaker's commitment to presupposed content is a matter of degree. In our examples, it seems plausible to maintain that the speaker's commitment to the presupposed content in (1) and (2) is somewhat stronger compared with the commitment to the presupposition in (3). That seems correct. We should also note, however, that some presuppositions are more context sensitive than others. Consider (3) again: in some conversational contexts, it might be important to the conversation whether the person spoken about is married to John or not, and, in other contexts of conversation, it

[11] S. Soames, "Presupposition," in *Philosophical Essays, Vol. 1* at 573.

[12] I take it that it is possible for an agent to regret that P, even if P has not actually occurred; it is impossible for an agent to regret that P, however, if the agent does not *believe* that P occurred.

might be quite immaterial. At least in part, this context sensitivity can be seen by looking at those cases in which the presupposed content turns out to be false, and then ask how that falsehood would affect the content that the speaker managed to convey. Suppose, for example, that it turns out that John is not married. Would it necessarily defeat the main content of the speaker's utterance of (3)? That depends on circumstances: if both speaker and hearer knew the identity of the woman spoken about, and simply wanted to refer to that person, then the fact that she is not really married to John would have made little difference to the main content of the utterance. On the other hand, with respect to utterances like (1) or (2), it would be much more difficult to think of any context where the falsehood of the presupposition would not defeat the main content of the utterance. This follows from the fact that some presuppositions are particularly sensitive to the context of the conversation, and others are less so.

c. Semantically encoded implications

Grice suggested in a few famously cryptic remarks that there are cases in which implicated content follows from *the meaning* of the words used in the expression uttered. Implicated content is often *semantically encoded* in the expression that the speaker used. Grice called them *conventional* implicatures.[13] However, the same phenomenon is often present in utterance presuppositions as well. In both cases, certain content might be implicated in a way that is semantically encoded in the expression uttered by the speaker.[14] So let us look at some examples, disregarding, for now, the distinction between implicatures and presuppositions. Consider the following utterances:

(4) "Even X can A" (implicating that there are some others, besides X, who can A, and that X is one of the least likely among them to A).

(5) "X managed to find A" (implicating that finding A was expected to involve some difficulty).

(6) "It was X who broke the vase" (implicating that somebody must have broken the vase).

[13] P. Grice, *Studies in the Way of Words* at 25. The question of whether there is anything really conventional about such semantically encoded implications is a question I have dealt with elsewhere: A. Marmor, *Social Conventions* at ch. 5.

[14] Indeed, L. Karttunen and S. Peters have argued that utterance presuppositions just are conventional implicatures; see their "Conventional Implicatures." I do not quite agree with their view (*Social Conventions* at 115), but this disagreement does not affect my arguments in this chapter.

(7) "X is not coming to the party tonight" (implicating that there must have been some expectation that X would/might come to the party tonight).

(8) "The Republicans and Senator X voted against the bill" (implicating that X is not a Republican).

(9) "I cannot join you for dinner; I have to meet with X" (implicating that the two events in question—the dinner and the meeting with X—overlap in time).

Common to utterances (4)–(9) is that, in addition to the assertive content of the utterance, some content is implicated by the speech, as indicated in the parenthetical text. There is, however, this crucial difference: in the utterances of (4), (5), and (6), the relevant implicated content is semantically *encoded* in the expression used. This is clearly manifested by the fact that the implied content is not cancelable by the speaker. It simply makes no sense to say that "it was X who broke the vase" and then immediately try to cancel the implication/presupposition by saying that actually nobody broke the vase.[15] On the other hand, the relevant implications in (7), (8), and (9) are not semantically encoded. And again, this is attested to by the fact that the implied content is cancelable by the speaker. For example, there can be a context in which it would make sense to express (8), even if X is also a Republican. It could have been a known fact, shared by the conversational parties, that Senator X was widely expected to vote for the bill. By saying that the "Republicans and X" voted against the bill, one may be clarifying something that the conversational parties would have found informative and relevant, given their specific background expectations.[16]

Generally speaking, I will assume here that cancelability is a sound criterion for distinguishing between implicated content that

[15] Notice that semantically encoded implications are typically projectable: the implication remains even when the expression is embedded in negations, conditionals, etc. (anaphora might be an exception, though. See the note below.).

[16] Note that a semantically encoded implication does not necessarily follow from the meaning of individual words; in some cases, different content is implicated by the same word used in different types of sentences. As an example, compare the implication of the word "too" in these two cases of anaphora: "Joseph was in the room, *too*" (implicating that others were in the room), and "If Joseph goes to the meeting, the department chair will be there, *too*" (implicating that Joseph is not the department chair). The example—though not quite the point of it—is taken from Kripke's "Presupposition and Anaphora." This is also discussed in my *Social Conventions* at 113.

is semantically encoded and content implicated that is not semantically encoded. If the implication of an utterance is not cancelable, it is because the implication is semantically encoded in the expression uttered. By choosing to use a certain expression, the speaker has already committed himself to the content that is implicated by the meaning of that expression. Implications that are not semantically encoded are such that their content is inferred from the combination of the expression used in a given conversational context and some conversational norms (maxims, in Grice's terminology) that the speaker is presumed to follow.

Admittedly, however, the distinction between implications that are semantically encoded and those that are only triggered by the semantics of the expression is not always so easy to discern. Consider, for example, a speaker S uttering the following sentence:

(10) "All Xs who are F ought to φ."

There is a clear sense that in uttering (10), the speaker, S, is committed to the content that *there might be an X who is not F*. Is this an implication that is semantically encoded in (10)? Not entirely. What (10) implies is something like this: *for all that S knows* (in the context of this utterance), there might be an X who is not F. Why is that? Arguably, because otherwise S would have violated the maxim of quantity (do not say too little). Had S *known* that all Xs are Fs, his utterance would have expressed too weak a proposition—it would have said too little, as it were. Therefore, we may safely conclude from the utterance of (10) that for all the speaker knows, there might be an X that is not F. But this implication partly depends on the Gricean maxim of quantity; it is generated by some pragmatic features of the speech. What we have here, I think, is some information that is triggered by the expression used that, together with the assumption that the speaker adheres to the maxim of quantity, generates a certain implicature. It is a case of a *generalized conversational implicature*.

2. Strategic Speech

As we noted in the previous section, the paradigm of an ordinary conversation in the Gricean model is based on the assumption that the parties to the conversation are engaged in a cooperative exchange of information. The maxims discussed above are essentially derived from this cooperative principle; they are the norms that we would expect speakers and hearers to follow in light of the general cooperative purpose of the conversation. Grice realized, of course, that not all speech situations are cooperative exchanges of information.[17] In some cases, the point of the conversation is not the exchange of information. Consider, for example, expressions we use in the context of courtesy or politeness. These are cases in which some form of cooperation certainly dominates, but not typically of the kind that involves a truthful exchange of information. A polite remark or an expression of courtesy is not meant to be entirely truthful or implicate anything beyond what is conventionally regarded as appropriate. When the host of the dinner party you attend asks you how you liked the food, you are expected to retort something nice and appreciative, not necessarily the truth. (Perhaps in such cases there is a certain expectation to pretend that you say something true, even if the commitment is not to the truth of what you say. I am not sure—sometimes there is not even a pretense, just an expectation to comply with a convention or a ritual.)

Polite conversations are cooperative, even if they are not truthful exchanges of information. Other types of conversation, however, are less cooperative. Presumably, some element of cooperation is necessary for any communicative interaction. It is difficult to imagine a conversation in which the speaker would entirely flout the maxim of relevance, for example. But the level of cooperation is subject to variations, depending on the purposes of the conversation and its general context. It would be terribly naïve, for example, to assume that a car dealer trying to sell you a used car is going to adhere to the maxims of quantity, not telling you too little or too much.

The limiting case of noncooperative implicature is manipulation. These are cases in which a speaker asserts something true while deliberately trying to implicate something that he knows to be false. As an example, consider this case: Mr. Smith goes to a hospital and, in making some enquiries with one of the nurses, presents himself as "Dr. Smith." As it happens, Smith's doctorate is in philosophy. Wouldn't the nurse be rather surprised, and quite rightly annoyed, in learning this little detail later? True, Mr. Smith did *not assert* that he is a medical doctor but, given the circumstances, it is an implication that

[17] Grice mentioned some possible modifications of the cooperative principle concerning polite conversations and utterances aimed to direct or influence the actions of others. His discussion of these modifications is rather sketchy, however, and does not address the possibility of strategic conversations discussed here. *Studies in the Way of Words* at 28–30.

would naturally follow. In other words, the asserted content here is true; it is only the implicature that is false. Such cases of manipulative speech show that an implicature can be abused. But notice that the abuse or manipulation is made possible precisely because the hearer wrongly assumes that the speaker adheres to the ordinary Gricean conversational maxims.

Legislation is not a form of manipulative speech. But it is not fully cooperative either. The kind of discourse we often have in the legal case is *strategic* in nature. The essential feature of strategic speech—as I will use the term here—is that the speaker strives to gain some advantage by implicating more (or less) than he would be willing to make explicit. In an ordinary conversation, although the speaker does not have to make explicit what his utterance conversationally implicates, we assume that the speaker would be willing to explicitly acknowledge the relevant implicature. Explicating the implied content would not defeat the purpose of his utterance. But this is precisely the element that differs in strategic speech: the speaker tries to implicate something that she is not quite willing to make explicit, precisely because it might defeat the purpose of her implication. Insinuation is a clear example. Suppose that by saying X in context C, the speaker intends to insinuate to H that Y. Rendering Y explicit, by stating it or affirming it, defeats the purpose of the utterance as a form of insinuation; it is no longer an insinuation if you actually assert it. It is an essential aspect of insinuating something, as opposed to stating it, that some content hangs in the air, as it were, implied but not quite stated—that is, you suggest something without a full willingness to assert it.[18]

To be sure, I am not suggesting that insinuation is necessarily or even typically strategic speech. It may be, depending on the larger context of the conversation. What makes a speech strategic is the fact that the speaker aims to gain some advantage by implicating certain content that he would not be willing to express or acknowledge explicitly.

This element of less than full commitment to the content implicated is not confined to the speaker. Hearers can be similarly situated in not being willing to fully acknowledge the uptake of content that goes beyond what is explicitly asserted. In various situations, hearers

[18] See P. Strawson, "Intention and Convention in Speech Acts." We should keep in mind that speakers may have many kinds of reasons for preferring to implicate rather than actually say something. I am not denying this. But the point in the text is that, in only certain types of cases, explicit acknowledgement of the implicature would defeat the kind of speech act the speaker intended to engage in. Insinuation is one such case.

purport to maintain a kind of plausible deniability—that is, the ability not to acknowledge full uptake beyond what is actually asserted. Children are particularly known to take advantage of uptake deniability when they want something that is not explicitly prohibited. Consider this familiar example: Bob the eight-year-old wants some chocolate, and his mother says: "You just had a bunch of candy an hour ago!," clearly implicating that chocolate now is out of the question. Bob goes ahead and gets the chocolate anyway, and when asked to account for his misconduct, he says: "But Mom, you *didn't say* that I could not have it!," which is true, of course; she did not say that. Deniability of implicated uptake is not confined to childish behavior, of course. In fact, it is one of the official dogmas of criminal law that conduct that is not explicitly prohibited (viz., stated, asserted) cannot amount to a criminal offense. Whether this dogma is practically adhered to is questionable, but that is a separate issue.

Consider another example of strategic speech, and one that is familiar to us in the academic context, about the ways in which we read letters of recommendation.[19] Suppose that you are considering a job candidate who just finished her PhD at another university, and you are reading the letters of recommendation written by her professors. Naturally, you are interested not just in what the letter explicitly asserts but, perhaps even more so, in what the content of the letter implies. You try to read, as it were, between the lines. But you also suspect that the recommender, interested as he may be in the promotion of his student, might try to imply a bit too much. So you try to figure out the implications of what you read in the letter, but you take it with a grain of salt. And, of course, the colleague who wrote the letter knows all this, and you know that he does. So how does it work? What is it about strategic forms of communication that enable speakers to implicate some content that they would not be willing to make explicit, or hearers to be able to deny uptake that goes beyond the asserted content?

Generally speaking, I would suggest that strategic communication works when there is a certain level of uncertainty about the normative framework that governs the conversation. In ordinary conversations, when parties aim at a cooperative exchange of information, the normative framework is fairly robust, requiring speakers (and hearers) to adhere to the Gricean maxims of relevance, truthfulness, quantity, and manner. As we mentioned earlier, the maxims directly

[19] Famously one of Grice's examples, though not in the context of strategic speech.

instantiate the purpose of the conversation as a cooperative interaction. When the conversation is not entirely cooperative, however, the maxims are not entirely adhered to; parties to the conversation are not fully committed to following the cooperative maxims, either because it is not entirely clear that a certain maxim applies, or because it is not entirely certain that parties are expected to strictly adhere to the pertinent maxim. In other words, two kinds of uncertainty enable strategic moves in a conversation. In one type of case, it is not entirely clear whether a given maxim applies or not. For example, am I really expected to tell the truth when the waiter in a restaurant asks me whether I like the food? Or when my wife asks me whether I like the expensive new dress she just bought yesterday? It is pretty clear that there is some doubt about the requirement of truthfulness here: on the one hand, it is far from obvious that I am expected to commit to the truth of what I reply; on the other hand, it cannot be entirely clear that I am not expected to say the truth, otherwise why bother to ask? The maxim of truthfulness hangs in the air here, so to speak, without obviously applying or obviously not applying.

The second kind of uncertainty concerns the level of compliance with a given maxim that would normally apply. Consider, for example, a stipulation in some commercial contract saying that "X will not issue A without Y's proof of B." In an ordinary conversation, a hearer would have inferred that proof of B is the only condition for X to issue A; otherwise, the speaker would have flouted the maxim of quantity (don't say too little). But in the context of commercial negotiations, this would be a very insecure inference. X might want to be able to claim that stating one condition does not necessarily preclude others, and Y might be expected to know this, to some extent, and to know that this might be what X presumes in the conversational context. But if it is obvious to both parties in the conversation that the maxim of quantity does not apply here, then X would not have been able to gain any advantage in implicating less than what would otherwise follow from his utterance; if a strategic move is possible here, it is only because the maxim of quantity is not entirely flouted but not entirely complied with either.

The example of the letters of recommendation we read and write about our students is another case in point. The maxims cannot be flouted in such contexts because writers try to take advantage of their ability to implicate some content beyond what the letter states or asserts. However, sometimes we want to implicate a bit less (or more) than we would be willing to state explicitly, and this can only be achieved if there is some level of uncertainty about compliance with the relevant maxims. "Don't say too much" is not a maxim strictly adhered to in such contexts. Sometimes we say too much—e.g., go on and on about the content of the student's dissertation—precisely in order to implicate less (about the actual talents and abilities of the student).

To sum up so far: two main features of strategic communication distinguish it from an ordinary cooperative exchange of information. First, there is typically a certain misalignment of interests: a speaker's interest in implicating a certain content and the hearer's interest in acknowledging the uptake of that content might diverge, to some extent. The speaker wants to communicate more (or less) than she would be willing to make explicit, while the hearer may not have an interest in acknowledging the uptake of such oblique implications. The hearer's interest is often one of maintaining some plausible deniability of the uptake of the implication, acting *as if* he did not grasp or hear it. Second, this mixture of cooperative and noncooperative elements of strategic communication is made possible by a certain degree of uncertainty about adherence to the maxims of conversation. The lack of certainty about the normative framework leaves some content hanging in the air, as it were, leaving each party to the conversation with an option of understanding the full communicated content somewhat differently.

Admittedly, all of this is very general and imprecise. We need to see how these features of strategic communication actually work. In the next section, I will examine some key features of legislative speech to demonstrate the strategic nature of legal communication. The account is not meant to be exhaustive. My purpose is to demonstrate some of the difficulties and their possible solutions.

Before we examine the various complexities that are present in the legal case, however, let us return to the kind of implications that are semantically encoded. I think that we can safely maintain that implications that are semantically encoded inevitably form part of the content of the law. Precisely because such implications are not cancelable, and they do not normally depend on the particular context of the conversation, we can assume that if an instance of legislative speech saying that P semantically implicates that Q, then Q is part of what the legislative speech actually determines as a matter of communicative content. In other words, semantically encoded implications are basically on par with assertive content.

To be sure, I am not suggesting that a speaker is committed to all of the content that is logically or otherwise *entailed* by what he says. People cannot be expected to be committed to content that they could not be aware of.[20] Generally speaking, however, speakers can be taken to be committed to content that is *obviously and transparently* implicated by the semantic features of the expression they have uttered, given normal linguistic competence in the relevant natural language.

Is there any reason to doubt that semantically encoded implications are necessarily part of the law's communicated content? If there is any doubt about this, it might stem from the relative lack of specificity of the implied content. Content that is implied by the kind of expressions under consideration here is often somewhat unspecified. The specification of such content is typically context-dependent. Nevertheless, even if the relevant expression leaves some content unspecified, the information encoded might be sufficient to make a difference. If a speaker asserts, for example, that "Even John can pass the exam," the speaker is clearly committed to the following content: (i) that there are others, besides John, in some relevant reference group, who can pass the exam; and (ii) that among those in this group, John is one of the least likely to be able to pass it. Of course, the hearers would need some contextual background to know what is the relevant reference group here. In this respect, the content is semantically underspecified. But the rest of the content in (i) and (ii) is semantically entailed by the use of the word "even" in this sentence, regardless of the particular context of this utterance. And this content is not cancelable. Imagine a speaker who says, "Even John can pass the exam; after all, he was the best student." This would be a very perplexing utterance; it is difficult to imagine a context in which it would make sense.

3. Strategic Speech in the Law

As I argued in the previous chapter, an act of legislation in a legislative assembly is a collective speech act, communicating some legal content that we take to be the law enacted. Clearly there are two main conversations going on in such a process. First is the conversation among

[20] Surely those who have used and expressed the axioms of arithmetic for centuries cannot be taken to have been committed, in any sense whatsoever, to the truth of Gödel's theorems, though, as we now know, Gödel's theorems are entailed by those axioms and some truths about set theory. I owe this example to Scott Soames.

the legislators themselves during the enactment process, and second is the result of this internal conversation as a form of collective speech addressed to the subjects of the law enacted, often mediated by the courts (or various agencies).[21] Now, of course, the internal conversation among legislatures is very strategic. It certainly does not abide by the Gricean maxims of a cooperative exchange of information. And then, when courts get to hear the legislative speech, as it were, it would be difficult for them to ignore the strategic nature of the conversation that generated the collective speech. Furthermore, this is not a one-sided conversation: the courts respond to the legislature by the ways in which they apply the law and interpret it in doubtful cases. And then the legislatures tend to respond to the courts in various ways, sometimes by overruling the courts' decisions, or by adjusting the legislative discourse to the courts' signals, and so forth. Generally, my assumption here is that both the legislatures and the courts have an inherent interest in maintaining a strategic form of communication in the ongoing discourse between them. The legislatures need the strategic discourse mostly in order to facilitate deals and compromises that are needed to get legislative results. And the courts need the strategic discourse mostly to gain greater control over legal results; the more strategic flexibility they have, the more power they can exercise, in the long run, over decisions they face.[22]

Let me mention some familiar examples to demonstrate these points, and then try to draw some general conclusions. The most familiar aspect of legislation is that it is almost always a result of a compromise. Compromise often consists in what I would like to call *tacitly acknowledged incomplete decisions*—that is, decisions that deliberately leave certain issues undecided.[23] This is closely tied to the fact that legislation is an instance of collective agency:

X would want to say that "P," intending to implicate Q.

Y would want to say that "P," intending to implicate not-Q.

[21] Actually, the situation might be more complicated because sometimes the legislature purports to convey different messages to different audiences. This general phenomenon of legislative double-talk is familiar from Meir Dan-Cohen's work on acoustic separation in criminal law ("Decision Rules and Conduct Rules."). I have tried to explain the linguistic relevance of such double-talk in my "Pragmatics of Legal Language."

[22] There is, probably, a great deal of strategic conversation going on between the judges themselves in appellate courts. The decision procedures and the culture of decision-making on higher courts vary considerably between different jurisdictions, and thus may be difficult to generalize.

[23] There is nothing new in this idea; it has been noted by numerous writers.

> X and Y act collectively, *intending their collective speech in saying "P"* to remain undecided about the implication of Q.

The general problem is that the underlined *intending* is often not so clear; in fact, the typical case would be one of conflicting and incompatible intentions, hopes, expectations, etc., viz., both X and Y intending—or hoping, or expecting—their intentions to prevail. In some cases, this may not be problematic: it is certainly possible that both X and Y would have conflicting intentions or expectations about the implication of Q, without intending their *collective* speech to implicate anything about Q. This kind of compromise is often achieved by settling on a wording in the bill that is vaguer than would be otherwise required. In such cases, the legislators basically agree to a delegation of power, leaving the specification of the vague term to be settled by the courts.[24] But it would be unrealistic to assume that this is always, or even typically, the case. More often than not, legislators would like to have their legislative agenda realized in practice; they would want to achieve certain goals that are better served by an application of the bill they enact in ways in which they want it to be understood. In other words, the typical case would be the one in which both X and Y expect or at least want that the *collective expression of "P"* would implicate (or not) that Q.

As an example, consider two legislators agreeing to the following formula of an anti-discrimination provision: "It is unlawful to discriminate against persons on the basis of gender, race, ethnicity, or nationality." Now suppose that one of the legislators assumed that "to discriminate against a person" clearly implies that discrimination would be unlawful if, and only if, it is *intentional*. But the other legislator may not have shared this intended implication. After all (she thought), people can engage in discriminatory practices even if they are not aware of the discriminatory effect of their conduct. And similar divergence can be present with respect to the question of whether the list of grounds for discrimination in the legal provision is exhaustive or not; does this law allow discrimination if it is not based on the listed grounds? (I will say more on this type of implication below.) Once again, it is certainly possible that the collective expression is intended to be indeterminate about these questions (which is typically tantamount to an intention to delegate the decision to

[24] This will be discussed in detail in chapter 4.

the courts). But it is equally possible that legislators simply intend to implicate different content by their collective expression.

Now, of course, when this kind of collective action involves numerous agents, sometimes hundreds of legislators, with different political agendas and intentions about bills they enact and different roles they play in the legislative process, the difficulties are evident. In Gricean terms, the problem in such cases is twofold. First, there is a considerable indeterminacy about *who* counts as a relevant party to the conversation—e.g., the initiators of the bill, the less-than-enthusiastic supporters, those who voted against?[25] And, second, there is an inherent uncertainty about *what* counts as a relevant contribution to the conversation that different parties are allowed to make. Remember that part of what enables legislators to reach compromises is the fact that they do not have to make their motives, intentions, or expectations evident.

Let me pause to take stock. I have tried to show that, unlike regular conversational contexts, where the parties to the conversation aim at a cooperative exchange of information, a partly noncooperative form of communication is present in the legislative context. The process of legislation itself is plagued with strategic behavior that tries to overcome the lack of initial cooperation between the relevant agents.[26] And then, once we have the result of this process, it becomes very difficult to determine which aspects of it are relevant to determining the implicated content of the legislative speech and which aspects ought to be ignored. Furthermore, these difficulties play into the hands of the courts, so to speak, because they enable the court itself to engage in strategic communication with the legislature, thus giving courts a greater power in determining legal results.

Assuming that I am correct about this, the following question arises: if the set of maxims of conversation that Grice identified does

[25] For an excellent analysis of the political dynamics of legislation and the differences between various groups of legislators, see D. B. Rodriguez and B. R. Weingast, "The Positive Political Theory of Legislative History."

[26] Admittedly, the more solid and monolithic the legislative majority is, the less strategic flexibility it may need. Thus, one might be tempted to think that, in legislatures with a solid one-party majority, particularly in parliamentary systems, strategic flexibility is not really needed. I agree that it is needed less; however, we should bear in mind that the culture of discourse between legislatures and the courts evolves over long stretches of time, and solid majorities today may find themselves in the minority tomorrow. In the long run, both parties would normally prefer to forgo some control over particular legal results in favor of more flexibility and thus more power in the future.

not necessarily apply to the context of legislative speech, are there other norms that apply instead? Or can we identify which of the Gricean maxims of conversation would apply to the kind of strategic behavior manifest in legislative speech situations, and which would not apply? The answer is rather complex: it partly depends on the normative—that is, moral-political—understanding of the role of legislation in a legal system, and partly on the interpretative practices that courts actually follow. However, as the argument in the previous section suggests, we should not expect such norms to be fully determinate in any case. Let me try to explain these points.

Abstractly, the idea is this: one might think that, just as we draw conclusions about the maxims that apply to an ordinary conversation from the basic cooperative objective of ordinary conversations, we should be able to draw some conclusions about the maxims that would apply to legislative speeches from the nature and objective of such communicative interactions. Can we not simply observe the main objectives of legislation and then draw some conclusions about the relevant conversational maxims that would instantiate those objectives? Perhaps we can think about it in a way that is very similar to a competitive game. Games typically manifest certain forms of strategic behavior. The rules of the game determine what counts as the point of the game, and what kind of skills and abilities one would need to exhibit to play the game and play it successfully. Typically we can draw some conclusions from the purpose of the game about different forms of conduct in it that would be deemed permissible, and others that would not be permissible. Consider chess, for example. Since it is an intellectual kind of competition, we should be able to conclude that chess players are not allowed to use physical intimidation as part of their tactics in the game. In other games, however, such as boxing, and perhaps even football, physical intimidation might be perfectly acceptable. In other words, we can draw some normative conclusions about the kind of moves players should be allowed to make simply from the nature of the game and its general purposes. Can we extend this analogy to legislation, and try to deduce some maxims of conversation that would instantiate our conception of what kind of "game" legislation is, so to speak?

Two main considerations count against such a possibility. First, the problem is that any conception of the nature of the "game" that would be sufficiently thick to generate the kind of normative conclusions we are after is bound to be controversial. People, including judges, of course, tend to have very different moral-political conceptions of the appropriate division of labor between legislative and adjudicative institutions in the relevant political system. There is, for example, a well-known debate about the role of legislative intent in statutory interpretation. People hold very different views about the appropriate roles of legislative intent in statutory interpretation, ranging from those who advocate great deference to intentions of legislators to those who hold the view that such intentions are completely irrelevant. Now, this is just an example of the kind of debate that reflects deeper controversies about the institutional role of a legislature in, say, a constitutional democracy. The question of whether we should take into account, and to what extent, the particular intentions of a legal-political authority in interpreting its directives partly depends on one's views about the legitimacy of such authorities, and their moral-political rationale.[27] And these views tend to be very controversial.

Furthermore, as I have tried to argue here all along, this kind of partial uncertainty about the norms that apply to legislative communication is not incidental. In fact, it is precisely a certain level of uncertainty about the relevant conversational norms that enables the parties to engage in a strategic form of conversation—that is, both during the enactment process and during the ongoing conversation between courts and the legislature. One caveat, however, needs to be mentioned. Over time, the norms of statutory interpretation that are actually followed by the courts may partly determine some conversational maxims of legislation. In following certain norms about the ways in which courts interpret statutory language, the courts could create some kind of Gricean maxims for the legislative context. For example, the extent to which courts are willing to hear evidence about statutory history would partly determine the norms of relevance about legislative implication. Such norms would partly determine what counts as a relevant contribution to the conversation between legislators and the courts, so to speak. Thus, to some extent, and greatly depending on the interpretative culture of the courts, some maxims of conversation might be specified for the legislative context.[28]

[27] I have explained this in much greater detail in my *Interpretation and Legal Theory*, ch. 8, and we will return to this in chapter 5.

[28] In the United States, courts have adopted numerous canons of statutory interpretation, some of which may look like quasi-Gricean maxims specific to legislative speech. See R. A. Carston, "Legal Texts and Canons of Construction: A View from Current Pragmatic Theory." (I will say more on this in chapter 5.) The problem is that these canons, numbering well over 100, often come into conflict, and thus the courts get to pick and choose which one prevails under the circumstances. Carston interprets me to argue

Note that the reliability of such norms crucially depends on the actual consistency, over time, of the interpretative practices of the courts. If the courts do not consistently adhere to the relevant interpretative practices, the legislators would not have clear signals about what would count as a relevant contribution to the conversation between them and the courts and, therefore, inevitably, even between the legislators themselves. But again, if my argument about the uncertainty of norms of strategic conversation is correct, we should realize that neither the courts nor the legislature would necessarily have a strong incentive to have norms of interpretation that are followed very consistently.

In other words, we should acknowledge that both the courts and the legislatures have an interest in maintaining the possibility of strategic moves in the ongoing conversation they conduct. As we have seen, a certain level of uncertainty about the normative framework of the conversation is essential for allowing a form of strategic speech to go forward. Therefore, both the courts and the legislatures have an interest in maintaining a certain level of uncertainty about the maxims that apply to their ongoing conversation. Inconsistent and less-than-fully predictable application of conversational norms by the courts (acquiesced by the legislature), is probably the main mechanism that allows this uncertainty to be continuously maintained.

Let me give a couple of examples to demonstrate these points. Consider first this familiar example of implicatures in legislative speech: suppose that the law asserts, "All Xs ought to φ unless X is an F, a G, or an H." (Or, the more typical case, the law asserts, "All Xs ought to φ," followed by another section prescribing an explicit exemption to those who are F, G, or H.) Now, this kind of utterance would normally implicate that the mentioned exceptions are exhaustive—namely, that *all* Xs who are not (F or G or H) ought to φ. Note that this implicature is cancelable; the legislature can easily indicate that it does not consider the exceptions to be exhaustive. However, absent such indication, it would be natural to assume that the legislature has implicated that F, G, and H are the only

against the very possibility of conversational implicatures in law (Carston: "Legal Texts and Canons of Construction," 16ff), but that is not what I claim. I am not denying the possibility that some implicatures in law would work, or that some canons of construction, if consistently applied, would amount to a kind of Gricean maxim of conversation.

permissible exceptions to the requirement of Xs to φ. (This is an instance of a generalized conversational implicature.)

Every first-year law student learns, however, that courts are not very consistent in applying such implicatures. Judges tend to be rather skeptical, and perhaps rightly so, of the legislature's ability to determine in advance all of the possible justified exceptions to rules they enact. Sometimes, therefore—but, crucially, not always—courts simply ignore the implicature; they treat a list of exceptions as illustrative or incomplete rather than exhaustive.[29] In such cases, the courts are hearing, so to speak, the assertive content of the legislative speech while ignoring the communicative content that was not quite asserted but only implicated by it. And notice that part of what makes this possible is a certain level of uncertainty about the relevant maxims of conversation, uncertainty that is generated by the courts' selective and not-quite-predictable application of the relevant maxims (the maxim of quantity, in this case). Given the strategic interests of both parties in this interaction—namely, the courts and the legislatures—a certain level of uncertainty about the extent of the courts' willingness to infer implicatures is understandable. It allows both parties to make various strategic moves in this game, so to speak.

My second example is about presuppositions. One interesting pragmatic aspect of presuppositions, noted by Soames in the definition I cited above, is the phenomenon of accommodation. When a speaker utters a sentence in a given conversation, the speaker would normally assume that there is some content that is already shared by his hearers and therefore does not need to be asserted. However, sometimes an utterance involves a presupposition that adds some information to the conversational background—information not previously shared by the conversational parties. In such cases, the speaker acts on the assumption that his hearers would be willing to add the presupposed content, without objection, to their shared background. Consider, for example, the utterance of (2) "Sarah forgot to pick up Jane from the airport." It is quite possible that the hearer of this utterance was not aware of the fact, or may have not known, that Sarah *was supposed* to pick up Jane from the airport. If the speaker is willing to utter (2) as

[29] A famous case in point is *Holy Trinity Church v. United States* 143 U.S. 457 (1892), discussed in the previous chapter. The prohibition on importation of "labor or service of any kind" was qualified in the statute by a list of exceptions that did not include, however, clergymen. The court basically ignored the implication that the list of exceptions is exhaustive.

stated, it is because he would assume that the hearer is willing to add this information to her background knowledge without any particular difficulty. So *now* she knows that Sarah was supposed to pick up Jane from the airport, and she is willing to add this information to her background knowledge in this conversation.

In the legal case, however, accommodation does not always work so smoothly, and for understandable reasons. Let me illustrate this kind of accommodation failure with the famous case of *TVA v. Hill*.[30] This was a lengthy and complicated litigation about the construction of the Tellico Dam by the Tennessee Valley River Authority. Environmental organizations wanted to halt the construction of the dam, claiming that it would endanger the habitat of a small fish, called the snail darter, in violation of the newly enacted Endangered Species Act.[31] As it turned out, however, after the environmental issues had come to the public's attention, Congress continued to fund the construction of the dam in its annual appropriation bills. Now, one would have thought that if Congress appropriates funds to the construction of a certain project, the presupposition is that the project is legally authorized.[32] Nevertheless, the Supreme Court decided that these appropriation bills could not be taken to have implicated that Congress legally authorized the construction of the dam in the face of the environmental opposition that was salient by that time. In effect, the court refused to accommodate the information that was conveyed by the presupposed content of the appropriation bills. By refusing to accommodate this fairly obvious presupposition, the court explicitly ignored content that the legislative speech is committed to.[33] I am not suggesting that the court was wrong (or right) to do this; I mention this case only to demonstrate how the pragmatic commitments

[30] 437 U.S. (1978) 153.

[31] The protection of the snail darter was not quite the main reason for the opposition to the dam; the issues involved were very complex, partly environmental and partly economic.

[32] Even more clearly so, given that there was a looming, unsettled question about the application of the Endangered Species Act to the Tellico Dam, because the construction of the dam had started years before the act came into effect. Many legal commentators assumed at the time that the act should not be applied to projects that were under way by the time it came into effect.

[33] For more details on this case: M. D. McCubbins and D. B. Rodriguez "Canonical Construction and Statutory Revisionism." (I do not quite share the authors' negative view about the court's decision in this case. I do think that they are right, however, that the court relied on questionable information about the deliberative quality of appropriations procedures in Congress.)

of legislative speech—which were very clear in this case—do not necessarily form part of the uptake that the court is willing to accommodate, and perhaps legitimately so.

I wish to make another point by mentioning the TVA litigation: this is one of those cases in which the strategic nature of legislative speech is demonstrated very clearly. When Congress enacted the appropriation bills, it was already apparent that there was serious environmental opposition to the construction of the dam and that the construction might be halted if the snail darter were added to the endangered species list (as it was). However, instead of making the unpopular move of explicitly overruling the Endangered Species Act and authorizing the construction of the dam (or explicitly overruling the Fish and Wildlife Service's (FWS) decision to list the snail darter as an endangered species), Congress hoped to achieve the result more obliquely by continuing the appropriation of funds to the construction. One can only surmise that there was not enough support in Congress to face the environmentalists head-on. Now, as I have tried to argue here, the more strategic the nature of the relevant conversation, the more likely it is that the pragmatic commitments of speakers and the interests of hearers in the uptake of those commitments may diverge, which is to say that the divergence of interests between speakers and hearers about implied content is likely to vary according to differences in legal areas and the types of legislative speech that are characteristic of different types of legal regulation. The more strategic the legislative context is, the less we should expect to see an alignment of the speaker's intended implications and the hearer's interests in acknowledging the uptake of those implications.

For example, in areas of regulatory legislation, particularly in areas in which the regulation is based on expertise, it is less likely that courts will have an incentive to ignore pragmatic implications of legislative speech.[34] In fact, the TVA decision itself nicely demonstrates this. One way to see the dilemma here is in terms of a conflict between two different types of legislation: on the one hand, there was the Endangered Species Act and the ensuing regulatory decision of the FWS that added the snail darter to the list of endangered

[34] The U.S. Supreme Court explicitly recognizes greater deference to expert agency regulations. This is called the *Chevron* doctrine, based on the decision in *Chevron U.S.A. Inc. v. Natural Resources Defense Council Inc.* 467 U.S. 837 (1984). As commentators have noted, however, the *Chevron* doctrine is itself discriminately applied, depending on the level of confidence that courts have in the relative expertise of the agency in question.

species; on the other hand, there were the appropriation bills enacted by Congress. Basically, the court decided that the expert regulatory legislation prevails. Once again, my point here is not to justify the court's ruling; the point is to demonstrate that the courts are quite sensitive to the distinctions between different types of legislative speech, and that judges largely follow the principle that the more strategic the legislative context is, the less they are willing to hear more than what the speech actually asserts.

I hope that my discussion shows that, as a general policy, this makes a lot of sense, and not only for the courts but for the legislature as well. As long as both parties have an interest in maintaining a strategic conversation, both have an interest in some level of uncertainty about the norms governing their conversation. Expert agencies, on the other hand, are typically not in the business of making strategic moves; they are under much less pressure to conceal their strategic aims, and they need less strategic flexibility and more clarity. Therefore, in the case of agency regulations, we should expect greater alignment between the speaker's pragmatic commitments and the hearer's willingness to grasp those commitments as such. Thus, generally speaking, the more strategic the nature of the interaction, the more we should expect a divergence between what the speakers strive to implicate and what the hearers would be willing to uptake or accommodate. And vice versa: the less strategic the legislative context is, the closer it comes to the standard Gricean model of ordinary conversations.

3

Truth in Law

In discussing the determinants of assertive content in chapter 1, I left open the question of whether legal prescriptions, of the kind we would normally find in statutory law and other types of legal directives, can be seen as speech acts stating or asserting some truth-evaluable content. But this issue cannot be side stepped. It is, after all, the regular business of lawyers and judges to draw legal inferences. Many of those inferences look like an ordinary syllogism, whereby a conclusion is derived from some premises about the normative content of the law and statements describing facts or events. It is difficult to see how such inferences can be valid if the premises are not truth-apt, that is, if legal prescriptions have no truth-evaluable content. So this is the main issue I want to examine in this chapter; my topic here concerns the question of whether we can ascribe truth-value to what the law says, and what it takes to do so. As we will see, two separate issues are involved here. The immediate and most obvious concern is about whether legal prescriptions are statements with some propositional content. A solution to this problem forms the content of the first part of the chapter (sections 1–3). In the last part (section 4), I will explore some structural aspects of legal syllogism, suggesting that there is an interesting analogy between truth in law and truth in fiction.

1. Propositional Content of Exhortatives

An inference is valid only if the truth of its premises guarantees the truth of its conclusion. Therefore, no question of validity about an inference can arise if the premises consist of sentences or linguistic expressions that do not express a propositional, viz., truth-evaluable, content. On the face of it, however, linguistic expressions of particular legal contents—that is, the content of constitutional and statutory prescriptions, judicial decisions, agency regulations, and the like—are not propositions. Laws do not purport to describe an aspect of the world. They do not tell us how things are, or are not; they tell us, roughly, what to do, or what not to do. Thus, the question is whether prescriptive content of the kind we find in legal provisions is the kind of content that is truth-evaluable at all. And if it is not, then no inferences taking such prescriptions as premises can be valid.

Before we proceed, it is important to clarify what is at stake here. I am not suggesting that, in order to provide the logical framework for legal inferences, we must confine ourselves to standard propositional calculus. Logicians have developed systems of deontic logic allowing us to formalize the logical relations between propositions that contain deontic operators, such as obligation, permission, etc. But deontic logic, or any other axiomatic system we could devise to deal with such expressions, is not the solution to our problem, only a tool we can use later. Deontic logic offers us a formalized system to deal with prescriptive sentences, *assuming* that there is some sense in which they can be true (or false).[1] These logical tools do not give us an interpretation of what makes prescriptions or deontic statements truth-evaluable; they assume that such an interpretation is available. But it is precisely the availability of such an interpretation that is being challenged here. In other words, the challenge is to show how legal prescriptions can have truth-evaluable content. Once we have such an interpretation, we can then employ deontic logic to evaluate the logical relations between the relevant statements. So let me turn to this now.

The main plausibility of a skeptical position here can be seen by looking at statements expressed in the imperative mood. Imperative utterances, such as "Close the door!" and "Stand over there!" etc., are not the kind of utterances that describe anything; their function is to motivate conduct, and they would seem to have no truth-evaluable content. I am not suggesting, of course, that legal norms are typically formulated as imperatives. But their linguistic or communicative function is very similar. And they are similar in two ways. First, laws prescribe modes of behavior; they do not describe how things

[1] See J. Jorgensen, "Imperatives and Logic."

are (or are not). There is, of course, an enormous variety of ways in which laws are formulated. Very few legal regulations are formulated as standard imperatives. Laws grant rights of various kinds, impose obligations, grant various agents, private and public, powers to introduce normative changes in the law, and so on. The unifying element, however, is conduct guidance. In one way or another, legal norms and legal decisions purport to guide conduct for some purpose or other.[2]

Second, when the law requires you to do something, say, that you "ought to do φ in circumstance C," it purports to say that you ought to do φ, *and* that you ought to do it *because* the law says so. Legal requirements do not simply point out to their subjects reasons for actions that apply to them. They purport to create or impose those reasons by expressing the relevant requirement. You ought to do it because the law says so. And again, in this, laws are very similar to standard imperatives. Consider, for example, the difference between the following two statements:

(1) S saying to H: "You ought to give Sarah $100."

(2) S saying to H: "Give Sarah $100!"

Statements of type (1) are normally expressed to point out a reason for action that applies to H—that is, regardless of S's saying so. By expressing (1), S would normally be understood to have pointed out to H, or reminded him, as it were, that there is something that he ought to do—that is, give Sarah $100 (say, because he promised to do it or such). The speech act itself does not purport to make any difference to H's reasons for action (or, if you like, to the truth-value of (1)). The reason is claimed or assumed to be there, as it were, regardless of S's utterance or speech act. On the other hand, imperative expressions like (2) necessarily imply an expectation that H regard the expression of S's imperative as a reason for action. The fact that S had uttered (2) purports to make a difference to H's reasons for action.

Speech-act theorists have long recognized that there is a wide range of speech acts that are normally expressed in order to induce the hearer to perform a certain action (or refrain from action, of course),

[2] It is possible, of course, for some legal enactments to have no prescriptive content. Legislatures sometimes enact various declarative laws that have no conduct-guidance element in them, such as declaring a certain bird as the official "state bird," or something like that. Such laws, however, are pretty rare, and, in any case, quite tangential to law's main functions in society.

and by way of recognizing the speech act itself as a reason to do as ordered, requested, etc. These include commands, orders, requests, pleadings, invitations, questions, and others.[3] Following Austin (with a slight modification), I will call these kinds of performatives *exhortative speech acts* or *exhortatives*.[4] Such speech acts purport to motivate conduct on the part of the hearer by the very act of expressing the relevant utterance, expecting the hearer to recognize the utterance as a reason for action. As with other performatives, some background conditions might be needed to secure the felicity conditions, or the success, of the speech act in question. Sometimes these background conditions consist of social conventions or rules of an institution, but I do not assume that this is necessarily the case.[5]

Legal instructions are typically exhortatives. In fact, they are probably paradigmatic examples of exhortatives. The enactment of a legal requirement, or the official expression of a legal ruling (say, by a court or an administrative agency), is the kind of speech act that purport to motivate conduct on the part of the addressees by way of recognizing the speech act as providing them with reasons for action. It does not mean that all legal prescriptions are formulated in an imperative mood, of course, or even that they are formulated prescriptively. An expression might be an exhortative even if formulated as a simple descriptive statement. Saying, for example, "It is very cold in here," might well be a request from someone to close the window, depending, of course, on the conversational background and mutual knowledge of the relevant circumstances. Similarly, a legal descriptive statement such as, "It is a misdemeanor to φ in circumstances C," is not a description of how things are in the world, but rather, a prescription that one ought not to φ in C. And again, when the law says that you ought not to φ, it invariably implies that you ought not to φ, at least in part, because the law says so.

[3] For a very useful taxonomy of such speech acts, see K. Bach and R. M. Harnish, *Linguistic Communication and Speech Acts*, 47–55.

[4] Austin called them "exercitive" (*How to Do Things with Words*, 151), while Bach and Harnish labeled them, more sensibly perhaps, as "directives" (see their *Linguistic Communication and Speech Acts*, 47). I refrain from using Bach and Harnish's terminology because "directive" has become the standard way of referring to authoritative speech acts, and I want to keep to the broader category that includes speech acts that are not necessarily authoritative.

[5] On the question of whether performative speech acts necessarily rely on a conventional setting, there is an ongoing debate in the literature. I have weighed in on this debate in my *Social Conventions* at 118–30. In any case, not all performative speech acts are exhortatives.

Now, assuming that laws are typically exhortative speech acts, the relevant question becomes whether exhortatives have truth-values. One may doubt there is a problem here. For inferential purposes, it might be thought, we can just stipulate an operator, such as "*imperative that* ___," followed by the content of the relevant exhortative. Thus, for example, consider an imperative statement:

(3) (S to H): "Close the door."

Now, the idea is that we can assign truth-value to (3) by the formula:

imperative that {H closes the door}

Notice that the truth-value is not assigned to the content in brackets, since it would entail that the imperative is true if H closes the door and false if H does not, which is not what we are after; the truth-value of an imperative cannot depend on compliance with it. Furthermore, notice that something like an "ought" operator will not do, because an imperative might be true (if there is a sense in which it is), as such, even if it is false that one ought to do as instructed. Thus, the idea is that we assign truth-value to "*imperative that* ___," such that it is true if an imperative with the content that follows the operator has been issued or expressed, and false if not. For logical-inferential purposes, this should work. But we would still need some interpretation of what makes it the case that the relevant propositions are true (or false). Is it simply the fact that the imperative has been expressed? Maybe it is, but we need some explanation for why it is the case and under what conditions. In other words, we need an interpretation of the truth-*conditions* of such statements. The fact that we can translate imperative statements and, presumably, other types of exhortatives, to some truth-evaluable statements by stipulating some operator that can be assigned a truth-value does not answer our question. We need to know what it is that *warrants* ascribing truth (or falsehood) to exhortatives of various kinds.

For the sake of simplicity, I will henceforth focus on some simple exhortatives, like orders or commands expressed in the imperative mood. The assumption here is that if we can provide an interpretation of ascribing truth-values to imperatives, then, with suitable modifications, other types of exhortatives could be treated similarly. Now, a natural way to interpret the propositional content of imperatives is to suggest that such content is self-referential. When S says to H, "Close the door!," the propositional content expressed is about the wishes of S; it expresses something about the mental state of the speaker, such as, "S wants/wishes H to close the door and wants/wishes H to recognize the expression of this wish as a reason for H to comply." This is undoubtedly a propositional content, of the standard descriptive kind. The proposition refers to the speaker's state of mind. In other words, when people express a request or an order or such, they normally express a wish or desire that something happen and the expectation that the addressee sees the expression of the request or the order for what it is—namely, as a motivational reason to act in a certain way.[6] That is, at least, in standard cases. I will deal with some nonstandard examples shortly.

To be sure, I am not suggesting that the self-referential content is what the imperative semantically *means*; an imperative statement means what it states—namely, "Close the door," or "Pass me the salt," etc. In other words, imperative sentences are not semantically reducible to their self-referential propositional contents. The propositional content in play is what makes an imperative true, or false, as the case may be. But can it be false? If an imperative expresses self-referential propositional content, then every *sincere* expression of an imperative would constitute a true proposition. If by saying, "Close the door," I express the proposition that I want you to close the door (and I want you to recognize my expression of this order as a reason for you to do so), how can such propositional content turn out to be false? Presumably, under normal conversational assumptions and given some conditions of sincerity, it cannot. But this is not a serious worry. There are similar phenomena (identified by Lemmon and others[7]) of sentences rendered true by their expression alone, such as, "I'm talking to you right now," or, more interestingly, the expression of a promise. When a speaker says, under normal conditions, "I promise to φ," the speaker has made a statement that is true, and it is true in virtue of the fact that it has been uttered. It cannot turn out to be false, even if the speaker did not really intend to keep the promise. By saying, "I promise to φ" (in a standard conversational context), the speaker expressed the fact that

[6] The main difference between an order and a request consists in the difference in the kind of reasons for action that the expression is expected to generate. Orders purport to generate protected reasons for action (or obligations), whereas requests would normally be regarded as generating a regular reason for action. The details are not easy to work out, but they do not affect the present argument.

[7] See E. J. Lemmon, "On Sentences Verifiable by Their Use," and Bach and Harnish, "How Performatives Really Work."

she undertook a commitment and it is the undertaking of a commitment in virtue of expressing it, hence true.[8]

I am not suggesting that there is no room for failure. An expression of an imperative may fail to convey a propositional content in the circumstances of its utterance. The order to close the door, for instance, presupposes that there is a door in the vicinity to be closed; if the presupposition is obviously false (say, I ask you to close the door while taking a walk in a meadow, with no door anywhere around), then it is quite possible that the utterance fails to convey a meaningful propositional content. I think that this is typically a pragmatic failure: we know what the sentence means and what it would take for it to be true; the failure consists in lack of relevance. The speaker uttered something that is not relevant to the conversational situation. But perhaps there are other ways to explain what kind of failure is involved here. I will not insist on this.

To sum up so far, the suggestion is that, in standard cases, an imperative statement expresses some propositional content about the speaker's intentions, wishes, or desires that is typically rendered true by its expression alone. With some appropriate modifications, this is true of exhortatives in general. Exhortatives are the kinds of speech acts by which the speaker intends to motivate some action (or inaction, of course) on the part of the hearer by way of recognizing the expression as a motivating reason for action. It is a crucially important feature of exhortatives that the first-person pronoun is always implicit in the expression of the exhortative; it always makes a difference who the speaker is, so to speak. When I make a request, for example, it is an essential feature of the expression that it is my request, that it expresses my wishes, intentions, or such.[9] Though rarely made explicit, the first-person pronoun is what the exhortative is about, as it were; it makes a quasi-descriptive statement about the speaker's state of mind. We can see evidence of this by juxtaposing an exhortative with the negation of its conveyed propositional content. Thus consider the following pairs of statements:

(a) "Close the door" *and* "It is not true that I express a wish that you close the door."

[8] I have explained this in greater detail in my *Social Conventions*, 120 ff.

[9] There are cases, of course, when one can express the exhortative of another; I may have been ordered to order you to φ. I do not think that such cases pose any particular problems. Typically, the second order is a description of the first; the utterance serves as a means of conveying somebody else's wishes, etc.

(b) "Please lend me $10" *and* "It is not true that I express a wish to borrow $10 from you."
(c) "You may leave the room now" *and* "It is not true that I express an intention to have/let you leave the room now."

As these pairs of conjunctions show, the juxtaposition of an exhortative with the negation of its conveyed propositional content, referring to the speaker's expressed state of mind, makes no sense. The conjunctions are incoherent or, at best, perplexing. The expression of an exhortative conveys a certain propositional content that cannot be contradicted without assuming that the exhortative has not been expressed sincerely. When you express an exhortative, *under normal circumstances and sincerely*, you have expressed some propositional content that is rendered true by its expression alone. Once again, I am not suggesting that exhortatives are semantically reducible to the propositional content they express. The suggestion is that such content follows from the kind of speech act that exhortatives are and their communicative function. The whole point of an exhortative is to get the hearer to recognize the speaker's state of mind and thereby motivate the hearer to act in certain ways. Exhortatives differ, of course, in the ways in which the speaker's intentions or wishes, etc., are taken to be reasons for action and the kind of reasons they are.[10]

All of this is true in standard cases, where exhortatives are expressed sincerely and the speaker means what she says. But this is not always the case. There are some nonstandard cases where the content communicated by an exhortative speech act implicates (or aims to implicate) something different from what it says. Consider, for example, Susan telling her husband, Bob, "Sure, you can go to the football game tonight. I don't mind." Let us assume, however, that Susan does mind, actually, and would much prefer that Bob stay at home with her. There are two ways to deal with such cases, depending on the nuances of the conversational context and similar pragmatic factors. One possibility here is that the condition of sincerity is not fulfilled. Susan's expression was not made sincerely. She expressed a permissive speech act but without the requisite sincerity. Another possibility,

[10] In fact, they may differ in other respects as well. For example, some exhortative speech acts, such as a command or a prohibition, typically presuppose some particular standing of the speaker vis-à-vis the hearer, such as an authoritative position, while others may not require/presuppose any particular standing. See Bach and Harnish, *Linguistic Communication and Speech Acts* at 47–55.

however, is that, in the context of this conversation, given background knowledge of the parties concerned, the expression conveys a different (actually the opposite) content from what the sentence literally means. And this is not unique to exhortative speech acts. As we saw in chapter 1, there are many instances in which people intend to assert something different from what they literally say, and normally this intention is easily recognized by the hearer. As with other forms of linguistic expression, the assertive content may be affected by various pragmatic features of the conversational situation and in ways that make the content asserted by the utterance different from what it literally states.

Admittedly, there are more complicated cases as well. Suppose, in our example above, that Susan's permission to let Bob go to the football game does assert what she literally says, and, thus, it does convey an intention to let Bob go to the football game, but, in fact, Susan also hopes (perhaps against all odds) that Bob will not go.[11] Can we say that Susan's permissive speech act expresses her wish or intention that Bob go to the game? That would seem to be incorrect, because we assume that she actually entertains the wish or the hope that he not go. This is a tricky case, but I think the plausible solution here is to maintain that Susan's communication intentions are in conflict with her hopes or desires. In other words, I think that Susan's exhortative speech act does express the propositional content that she intends to let Bob go to the game, though she hopes that the opposite will happen. And this is not totally irrational, nor unique to exhortatives. A similar problem is familiar from cases in which an agent tries to do something that he knows he cannot do, or tries to do something because he was told to do it and hopes to show that he cannot. For those who hold the view that trying to do something necessarily involves intending to do it, a similar type of conflict is present in such cases. The intention is in conflict with a hope or an expectation or such. Needless to say, this is not the place to deal with intentions to try and how to accommodate these counterexamples.[12] My point is that it is not necessarily irrational to express a wish or intention that is in conflict with a hope or desire; some exhortative speech acts may involve such conflicts. People can intend to convey one thing and

[11] Or, here is a similar example: I tell you, "Go ahead! Punch me in the nose!," hoping, of course, that you will not do so.

[12] See, e.g., G. Yaffe, *Attempts*, ch. 2.

hope that the opposite happens. The propositional content, however, is not determined by hopes or desires that accompany the expression. The fact that the speaker entertains hopes or expectations that differ from what she asserts does not, by itself, affect the truth-evaluable propositional content she conveys.

2. Truth-Evaluable Content of Laws

Let us now return to the legal context. When I ask you to close the door, I express a complex wish: I express my wish that you close the door and my wish that you recognize my expression of this wish as a reason to do so. The suggestion so far has been that the propositional content of exhortative utterances consists in the appropriate description of this complex state of mind. Now suppose that the context is slightly different. There is a sign on the entrance door to our department's main office saying, "No entrance after 6 p.m." Let us regard this sign as a kind of legal or quasi-legal instruction. Well, what makes it a kind of legal instruction? Presumably, the fact that whoever put up that sign was authorized to do so. Suppose it is the department chair. In terms of the propositional content of the instruction, there is no difference between the chair's instruction conveyed by the sign on the door and his instruction expressed orally, to each one of us one by one. Imagine that, instead of putting up the sign, the department chair stood there and issued the same instruction to each of us orally. The propositional content would be exactly the same. It is, of course, just much more efficient to convey that content by putting up the sign.

Now, it is possible, of course, that, personally, the department chair could not care less whether anyone is allowed to enter the office after 6 p.m. The instruction reflects his official wish, not necessarily his personal one. There is nothing unusual about that; people often express a certain content in their official roles that may not reflect anything they personally believe or wish. And this phenomenon is not unique to exhortatives or authoritative roles. For example, customer representatives you phone would often tell you that they thank you for your call and appreciate your business. They do not mean to speak for themselves, but for the company they represent. And, of course, you would be terribly mistaken to assume otherwise. The same holds for legal and other official authorities. They do not necessarily speak for themselves, personally, that is. Official exhortatives reflect, as they should, the wishes and intentions of persons in their official roles, qua officials, and this is normally how we understand such locutions.[13]

Let us take this one step further. Suppose that for some reason the issue is somewhat controversial in the department. Thus, the department chair holds a department meeting about this little controversy, and, after some back and forth, a resolution is reached not to allow people to enter the office after 6 p.m. and thus the sign is put up. Would this make any difference with respect to the propositional content of the instruction? Whether the instruction expresses the view of a single "legislator," so to speak, or a collective decision of a multitude, should not make a difference to what the propositional content of it is. But what if different members of the department meant slightly different things when they voted for the resolution? Perhaps some of them thought that the instruction only applies to students, while others assumed that it applies to faculty members as well. These are two different contents, both (let us assume) consistent with an ordinary understanding of the instruction under the relevant circumstances. Which one is it? Can we tell?

Here's what we can say: exhortatives, just like any ordinary proposition, would have some propositional content that is determined by the relevant expression in the context of its utterance, and some content left undetermined or unspecified. Suppose, for example, that somebody points to a particular door and says:

(4) "That door cannot be opened."

Clearly, this is a descriptive sentence with some propositional content that is true or false. But the utterance also leaves some content undetermined; does it mean that the door is locked, or is it jammed? The proposition is consistent with both of these options and, by itself, it does not pick out either. (Unless, of course, the context of the utterance clarifies which option it is; for example, the utterance might have formed part of a conversation about the poor maintenance of the building, suggesting in this case that the proposition asserts that the door is jammed, not that it is locked.) And this is true of most utterances expressed in an ordinary conversation, whether the utterance is a straightforward proposition, an imperative, or some other kind of expression. Typically, some content is determined by the

[13] This is nicely explained by M. Dan-Cohen in "Interpreting Official Speech."

expression in the context of its utterance and some content may be left unspecified.[14]

But we have not yet answered the question. And the question is about the relevance of the intentions of the speakers. What we have in the case of the departmental decision, as in a typical case of legislation, is a form of a collective speech, whereby different participants have somewhat different communication intentions about the content of the collective expression. The question is whether these different states of mind affect the propositional content of the collective utterance or not. And here is where we might get in some trouble. In the case of an ordinary propositional statement, the propositional content expressed is typically determined by a combination of the meaning of the words (and syntax) uttered, and some pragmatic determinants in play, such as common knowledge of the relevant contextual background, presuppositions, the maxims governing the conversation, etc. As we saw in chapter 1, the speaker's intention or state of mind, *by itself*, does not necessarily determine what he said. In our example (4), the speaker may have intended to say that the door is locked. But it is not necessarily what he said. (Unless, of course, some particular contextual background makes it clear that it is what the speaker asserted.)

It might seem, however, that the case with exhortatives is different. If the propositional content of an exhortative is, as I suggest, self-referential, describing the speaker's state of mind, then one might have to conclude that the relevant state of mind is what *determines* the propositional content asserted. And this would be a problematic result. For example, it would entail that, in the example of the collective speech, where different participants have somewhat different intentions, wishes, etc., the propositional content would vary with the particular participants involved; that seems like a mess.

The conclusion does not follow, however. Just as people can fail to express the exact content of their communication intentions in the case of a regular propositional statement, so they can also fail to express the content they had wished to express in the case of exhortatives. The truth-evaluable propositional content consists in what *is said or asserted* by a speaker in a given context, not by what the speaker intended to say. I am not suggesting that communication intentions

[14] For a much more detailed analysis see, e.g., S. Soames, *Philosophical Essays, Vol. 1*, ch. 10. Note that I focus here on assertive content, and for simplicity's sake, do not discuss the kind of content that is implicated, though not quite asserted.

are irrelevant, far from it. Under normal circumstances, in an ordinary conversational context, it is precisely the communication intentions of the speaker that we try to grasp by figuring out what is said (and perhaps implicated, etc.). But again, as I argued in chapter 1, the assertive content of an utterance is determined by what *a reasonable hearer*, knowing the relevant conversational background and context, would infer about the speaker's communication intentions from the words or sentences uttered in that context. Any plausible conception of what assertive content is must make room for the possibility that a speaker can fail to assert by her utterance all that she intended to convey.

Now the question is whether this is different with exhortatives: if the propositional content of an exhortative consists in the appropriate description of the speaker's state of mind, does it mean that the speaker's overall intentions in expressing the exhortative statement are constitutive of the content asserted by it in the particular context of the utterance? The answer is negative. Some intentions are constitutive, of course, but not all. Suppose, for example, that a student walks into my office and I say to him, "Please close the door behind you." It would be surprising if the student concluded that my request was that he lock the door, even if, for some strange reason, it is precisely what I intended to ask. If I had that intention, I simply failed to convey it. The expression of an exhortative is not an invitation for the hearer to guess what the speaker intended. It is an expression of a wish, and just like any other expression, it can fail to convey the full content intended by the speaker.

So now you can see where I am heading: the same goes for collective speech. Not all of the intentions that participants to a collective speech might entertain with respect to its content are determinants of the content asserted by the collective expression, whether the expression is an exhortative or not. Collective speech, just like an individual's expression, can leave some relevant content unspecified. In this respect, exhortative speech acts are not different from straightforward utterances of propositions.[15]

[15] One might think that collective speech is different, because we might have cases in which the collective expression does not actually reflect anyone's intentions. Suppose, for example, that the participants in the faculty meeting had different views, some preferring that nobody be allowed in after 4 p.m., others only after 8 p.m., etc., and the final resolution is a compromise that does not reflect any particular person's wishes or preferences. But these kinds of examples are very misleading. As I argued in chapter 1, once a proposition is put to a vote and gains majority support, then, at the very least, it gains the collective intention of the majority that it be adopted, which is to say, there is a collective

Let me add an important clarification: the discussion above is confined to the question of what is the asserted, truth-evaluable content of exhortatives. It does not have any direct bearing on the question of how to interpret such expressions when some doubts arise about their contents or their application to some problematic case. The latter crucially depends on the hearer's relevant interests or, more precisely, the reasons to pay attention to the utterance. It is quite possible that a hearer would be interested in, or have reasons to figure out, the speaker's intentions, hopes, expectations, etc., even if they were not quite asserted—or even implicated—by the speaker in the context of the utterance. We often want to know more than what the speaker said or asserted (or implicated). And even in the legal context, such knowledge might be quite relevant to the correct interpretation of the law. But these issues go beyond the focus of this chapter. I do not propose a theory of legal interpretation here. My only concern is to provide an account of legal speech acts that would allow us to ascribe truth-values to the contents expressed by them. How to complete such content when it is unspecified by the relevant utterance is a separate and much broader issue, involving many considerations that will not be discussed here.

3. Imperatives without Imperator?

Many legal philosophers and legal scholars reject the view that the content of the law is determined by the intentions of the lawmakers. There are many variants of such views, and some of them are clearly not relevant to our present discussion. In particular, the age-old debate about the potential relevance of legislative intent in statutory and constitutional interpretation is not about the question of what constitutes the propositional content of legal norms. It is a debate about how to interpret the law—that is, complete it—when some relevant issue is left under-determined or unspecified by the pertinent legal norm in question. As I said in the concluding remarks of the previous section, this is a debate that is not affected by the issues under consideration in this chapter.[16]

communication intention expressed by the resolution voted on. The fact that each one of the voters would rather have voted on a different resolution is beside the point.

[16] I will return to some of these issues in chapter 5.

The relevant objection to the thesis suggested here concerns the question of what it is that constitutes the truth-evaluable content of legal regulations. Some legal philosophers claim that, even when the content of a legal norm is clear enough, it is not clear because we know what the lawmakers intended to convey. The content of the law, they claim, is not determined by the communication intentions of its lawmakers. But again, it is important to distinguish between two very different, almost diametrically opposed, types of claims here. Some argue that law's overall content is not confined to norms that result from authoritative speech acts; norms or requirements can be legally valid and form part of the law, even if no authority has ever issued them (a view famously advocated by R. M. Dworkin). Others, however, concede that law is always a result of authoritative proclamations, but they deny that the content of those proclamations is determined by the communication intentions of the lawmakers. Both of these views, if correct, would raise some problems for the thesis I suggested in sections 2 and 3 of this chapter. So let me take them up, although in reverse order.

Textualism is taken to be the view holding that the content of a law is determined by what the law says, and not by what the lawmakers intended to say. As I will explain in chapter 5, textualism cannot be plausibly interpreted to maintain that the assertive content of a legal text is detachable from the communication intentions of the authority who issued the regulation. Generally speaking, understanding what someone said is precisely the attempt to understand what he or she intended to communicate. Textualists would be quite right to maintain, however, that assertive content is partly determined by some objective features of the conversational situation. What is said by an utterance consists in the kind of content that a reasonable hearer, sharing the relevant background knowledge, etc., can infer from the utterance in the context of its expression. The main import of textualism, however, is not about the question of what constitutes assertive content or what makes legal prescriptions true. Textualism's main point is about the ways in which legal content can be legitimately completed (by judges) when the relevant expression is incomplete or otherwise leaves some content unspecified. As I said earlier, this is a separate issue that I will discuss in chapter 5.

Now, at the other end of this debate, we find the view that denies, on general jurisprudential grounds, that law is confined to norms and regulations issued by legal authorities. According to Dworkin, for example, a certain normative content may form part of the law even if it does not emerge from an authoritative proclamation. Needless to say, this is not the place to present the full complexities of Dworkin's views about the nature of law and subject them to scrutiny. I have argued elsewhere, on grounds having nothing to do with the questions we have discussed here, that it is implausible to maintain that norms can gain legal validity without being authoritatively enacted as such. Only authoritative decisions make law.[17] However, for the purposes of the present discussion, it may be worthwhile to examine some aspects of this debate regardless of the wider jurisprudential issues involved. In other words, the question is whether we can have an exhortative content that does not express anyone's views about what ought to be done; are there imperatives without an imperator?

It might be tempting to think that the answer must be affirmative; after all, we do not think of moral norms or moral requirements as the kind of prescriptions that express anyone's wishes about what ought to be done. Or, at least, many philosophers think that this is the case, and I have no argument with that. So here is one way to see the difficulty. Take a certain prescriptive content, say:

(5) "A is required to φ in circumstances C."

Assume that it is both a legal requirement and a moral one. In other words, assume that the exact same conduct is both morally required and prescribed by a legal authority in a given legal system. Let's call them (5M) and (5L), respectively. Shouldn't one expect that the truth-evaluable propositional content of these two prescriptions, the moral and the legal, are to be exactly the same? After all, the conduct required by (5M) and (5L) is, ex hypothesi, identical.

The answer has to be negative; the propositional content of moral prescriptions is, essentially, different from that of legal prescriptions, even if the two prescriptions in question prescribe exactly the same kind of conduct. The truth of a moral requirement, I take it, has nothing to do with the views, intentions, or wishes of the person who expresses the requirement.[18] In saying that A is required (or should,

[17] See, e.g., R. M. Dworkin, *Law's Empire*, and my response in *Philosophy of Law*, ch. 4.

[18] Of course, some philosophers deny this; I am not arguing against expressivism here, just assuming that the objection comes from nonexpressivists. Expressivism, or any similar view about the nature of morality, would have no quarrel with the views I defend here.

or ought, etc.) to φ, one is typically pointing to the fact that A has reasons to φ, to some facts that count in favor of φ-ing, or such. But this cannot be the case with respect to the truth-evaluable content of a legal requirement. As we noted earlier, the expression of exhortatives is crucially different, in that it always invokes, albeit implicitly, the first-person pronoun; it matters who the speaker is. Whenever the law tells you to do something, it also tells you that you should do it because *the law* says so. And this is the sense in which legal prescriptions are paradigmatic examples of exhortative speech acts.

For another way to think about this, suppose, for example, that (5M) is true, and suppose that (5L) is the counterpart legal norm in a legal system S1, but not in a different legal system S2. Whatever else is the case, we should be able to explain in what sense (5L) is true if S1 governs and false if S2 governs, despite the fact that (5M) is true in both cases. In other words, whatever it is that would make (5M) true has nothing to do with the speaker who expresses it, whereas it is impossible to say whether (5L) is true or not without knowing who ordered (5L), in what context, etc.

Needless to say, this is not the place to suggest an analysis of the truth conditions or moral prescriptions. My only point here is that it is impossible to account for the truth-evaluable content of legal norms without reference to the origin or character of the norm as a legal one—namely, without taking into account that the same prescriptive content might be true in one legal system and/or at a given time and place, but not another. Law is one of those domains in which the *saying so* (by the appropriate agent under the appropriate circumstances) *makes it so*. In the next section, I explore another aspect of this phenomenon, with relation to a structural aspect of legal syllogisms.

4. The Lewis Fallacy

Let me begin with an analogy from truth in fiction. Sherlock Holmes, we are told in the Arthur Conan Doyle mysteries, lived at 221B Baker Street in London. Let us assume, therefore, that there is some sense in which (6) is true:

(6) Sherlock Holmes lived at 221B Baker Street, London.

David Lewis tells us that the building at 221B Baker Street in London at the time was a bank.[19] Let us therefore assume that, at the relevant times, (7) is true:

(7) The building at 221B Baker Street, London, is a bank.

The inference from (6) and (7) would seem to be:

(8) Sherlock Holmes lived in a bank.

But, of course, (8) is clearly false. What has gone wrong here? Lewis tells us that we made the mistake of moving from a *prefixed* to an *un-prefixed* context; (6) is true only if it is prefixed by an operator such as "In the fiction *F*..."; whereas (7) is true only if taken as un-prefixed (in the real world, as it were). Thus, unless (7) is prefixed by the same operator "in fiction *F*...," you cannot conclude that (8) is true in the fiction; and because (6) is true only if it is prefixed, you cannot conclude that (8) is true in an un-prefixed sense. Surely, this is quite right (and I will refer to this problem as the Lewis fallacy).[20] But now consider a legal example:

(6*) It is a misdemeanor, punishable by a fine of up to $100, to use a wireless telephone while driving a motor vehicle without a hands-free device.

(7*) John was talking on his wireless telephone, without a hands-free device, while driving his car.

The inference from (6*) and (7*) is:

(8*) John committed a misdemeanor punishable by a fine of up to $100.

[19] Or, as D. K. Lewis says, there may not have been a building there at all. See "Truth in Fiction," 262.

[20] See Lewis, "Truth in Fiction" at 262. A number of publications criticized Lewis's suggestions, though not on this particular point. See, for example, A. Byrne, "Truth in Fiction: The Story Continued." Some philosophers are inclined to deny that fiction has any straightforward propositional content. An alternative view (e.g., Kendal Walton's *Mimesis as Make-Believe*) regards fictional texts as invitations for the hearer to pretend that they believe what is said, or something along those lines. I am not claiming or assuming that these views are wrong. To account for what counts as propositional content of fiction we would need to tell a much more complicated story. None of this, however, affects my arguments here. I am only using truth in fiction as an example of a prefixed context.

Now, of course, the legal expression used in (6*), "It is a misdemeanor to φ..." should be construed here as an exhortative, actually expressing the prescriptive content that one ought not to φ, or something along those lines. Even so, the inference seems to be perfectly valid. In fact, it is the kind of inference that is characteristic of countless legal syllogisms. But on the face of it, we have committed here the Lewis fallacy of moving from a prefixed to an un-prefixed context: (6*) must be prefixed by an operator such as, "In the legal system *L*... (at time t, location x, etc.)...," whereas (7*) would seem to be un-prefixed; it is a straightforward description of an event that happened in the world. So how can we correctly infer (8*)? Notice that it does not help to construe (8*) itself as prefixed or contained under "In legal system *L*...," which is probably the right way to interpret the conclusion. Sherlock Holmes did not live in a bank either prefixed "in fiction *F*..." or un-prefixed. So if the inference about Holmes's lodging is unwarranted, so should be the inference about legal results such as (8*), whether the conclusion is understood as prefixed or not.[21]

Why should we think that (6*) must be taken to be prefixed? Although not expressed in these terms, the idea that sentences expressing the content of a legal norm refer to something that is true, if it is, only from a certain point of view—that is, from the perspective of a given legal system—has been widely accepted in jurisprudence, if not earlier, at least since Kelsen brought this to our attention.[22] In other words, a sentence like (6*) expresses a particular legal requirement or prescription that must be a requirement or prescription of a particular legal system in place. When people say that "X is the law," they necessarily mean to say that X is the law of some legal system or other at a given time and place. A given norm is a legal one if it forms part of a particular legal system and only as part of that system,

[21] It is tempting to think that the problem here is easily avoidable if we formulate the legal inference in conditional terms. We can reformulate (6*) as saying, "If X does φ, X is punishable..."; then (7*) can be construed as a statement to the effect that the antecedent obtains, and (8*) would thus follow as a valid conclusion. The problem is that this move avoids the problem only if (6*) is construed as a predictive statement and (8*) as a factual-predictive conclusion; otherwise, we are back to the same problem of mixing a prefixed conditional with an un-prefixed antecedent. Either way, as we shall see, the antecedent has to be incorporated into the prefixed context.

[22] H. Kelsen, of course, expressed this idea in terms of the necessity of presupposing the basic norm. See, e.g., H. Kelsen, *Pure Theory of Law*. Joseph Raz endorsed a similar view, expressed by his notion of "statements from a legal point of view"; see his *The Authority of Law* at 153–57. And see my *Philosophy of Law*, ch. 1, where I explain this in much greater detail.

at the time and place where it applies. Therefore, any statement that expresses the content of a particular legal requirement conforms to a formula that must be prefaced by, "*According to the law in S at time t...*" It makes no sense to talk about particular legal requirements or legal contents unless they are taken to be prefixed. Now, of course, there are many other ways to formulate this simple idea, without using Lewis's terminology. We can speak in terms of "true *in* S at time t..." or "it is the law in S at time t," or any other formulation that would express the same idea—namely, that the truth about the content of legal norms is necessarily relative to some system or other. This is what I mean by suggesting that legal statements are necessarily prefixed.

Now, you might think that there are prefixes that create a Lewis-type fallacy, and others that do not. And that is quite right. Let me call them *closed* and *open* prefixes, respectively. Open prefixes are such that they can occur in valid arguments with un-prefixed statements to yield valid conclusions. For example, "According to the laws of nature..."[23] So what is it about closed prefixes that they create the Lewis fallacy? One suggestion might be to look at the semantics of the prefix. It is probably implicit in the semantics of scientific prefixes—"According to the laws of nature..."—that they range over un-prefixed statements to yield valid conclusions. Whereas it is part of the meaning of a prefix such as, "according to fiction *F*..." that it ties the truth-value of the statement to be contained within a world demarcated by the prefix—that is, the world of fiction *F*. This is probably true, but it may not be enough. Still, you may wonder, what makes it the case that some prefixes are closed? My suggestion is that, at least in some central cases, prefixes are such that they designate a *constitutive relation* to the truth-values of the statements prefixed by them. A statement is true in a fiction, if it is, because the fiction states it. The saying so makes it true, so to speak. If a fictional text says that "the moon is green," then it is true, *in that fiction*, that the moon is green, and it is true *because the text says so*. Similarly, a prefix of a game, say, "according to [the rules of] chess it is the case that *p*," makes it the case that *p*, or that *p* is true, within the game. And, of course, *p* is true in chess (if it is) because its truth is constituted by the rules of the game.

In short, closed prefixes are those (but probably not only those) in which a constitutive relation obtains between certain essential

[23] According to some metaethical views, the same holds for "according to morality." But, of course, this is highly controversial in metaethics. Modal operators, such as, "it is necessarily the case that..." might be another example of open prefixes.

features of the world/context designated by the prefix, and the truths of the statements expressed about that world/context. So now I hope we can see why it would make sense to assume that the legal prefix is also closed. A certain legal content is true, if it is, in a given legal system S (at time t, etc.), because the law in S *says so*. A legal prefix, in other words, is closed because it ties the truth-values of statements prefixed by it to the world designated by the prefix itself. In this respect, law is very much like fiction, or structured games; saying so, in the appropriate ways, makes it so in the relevant context.

A natural solution to the Lewis fallacy in the legal case would be to maintain that the entire inference—(6*) to (8*)—is contained within the prefixed context, which is what makes the inference valid. The idea is that the minor premise, (7*), is also prefixed. In other words, (8*) follows as a valid conclusion only if (7*) is understood as prefixed by the operator, "According to the law in *S*..." If and only if the action committed by John amounts to "using a wireless telephone while driving" *from a legal point of view*, or *in the eyes of the law*, or such, then (8*) follows.

Before I try to explain this in greater detail, let us return to Sherlock Holmes for a moment. Consider the following inference:

(9) Sherlock Holmes lived in London.
(10) London is a city in the United Kingdom.
(11) Sherlock Holmes lived in the United Kingdom.

We have the same structure here as in (6) to (8), but a very different result. (9) is clearly prefixed by "In the fiction *F*...," whereas (10) seems to be un-prefixed; it is just a fact in the real world that London is in the UK. The conclusion, however, is quite right. Any sensible reader of the Conan Doyle mysteries would have assumed, and rightly so, that Sherlock Holmes's escapades take place in the UK.[24] And, crucially, this would be the case even if the United Kingdom (or England, or Great Britain) is never explicitly mentioned in the text. So what is it that makes the inference of (9) to (11) valid, as opposed to that of (6) to (8), which is not?

[24] I am not suggesting that it is impossible to offer an interpretation of the Holmes stories according to which they take place in a parallel universe, or on planet Krypton, etc., where London is not in the UK. I am suggesting, however, that those of us who assume that the Holmes mysteries take place in England would not be making any obvious mistake. And that's all we need for now. If you have doubts about the example, others can be thought of, e.g., that Sherlock Holmes had a nose or a brain, etc.

The solution has to be this: although (10) seems to be an un-prefixed proposition, in the context of this inference it is not; (10) is incorporated into the fiction by implication. The assumption here is that fictions typically incorporate by implication an indefinite, though limited, number of facts (or factual assumptions) about the world, at least those that are relevant, and can be assumed to be salient and well known to potential readers. Every reasonable reader of the Sherlock Holmes mysteries can be expected to know that London is a city in the UK, and, thus, even if the text does not mention this explicitly, it can be regarded as incorporating it by implication (assuming, of course, that there is nothing in the text to suggest otherwise). Thus we avoid the Lewis fallacy; the entire inference of (9) to (11) should be regarded as contained within the prefixed context. Similarly, even if the mysteries never refer to Sherlock Holmes's nose, we can assume that he had one (and only one), in virtue of the stated fictional fact that he is a man. These kinds of unmentioned facts can be said to be incorporated into the fiction by implication and thus, for inferential purposes, they can be regarded as prefixed statements.

Now let us return to the legal case. Can we similarly say that the inference from (6⋆) to (8⋆) is valid because (7⋆) is incorporated into the legal context by implication, and thus the inference as a whole is contained within the prefixed context? The difficulty with this solution is that it would require us to assume that all the facts in the world are incorporated into the law by implication and contained within its prefixed context. Since any fact or event in the world might be relevant to some legal inference or other, there cannot be a limit to the kind of facts that are contained within the prefixed context of the law. Notice that this is definitely not the case with fiction. There are countless inferences that would not be warranted about Sherlock Holmes, even if they rely on true facts (for example, consider our first example about the bank on Baker Street). In the case of fiction, we are willing to attribute some factual assumptions to be incorporated within the fictional world, as it were, only under certain conditions, such as certain assumptions of common knowledge, salience, relevance, lack of any contrary indication in the text, etc.[25] In the legal case, however, there seems to be no room for such constraints. This, again, would seem to suggest that we must assume that the law incorporates by implication all the actual facts in the world.

[25] These conditions can be controversial, of course. For example, in one of the Holmes stories, *The Adventure of the Speckled Band*, the culprit is a snake, a Russell's viper, that has

Now, there is a sense in which that is true, but to make it plausible, we must note a crucial constraint: facts have to be incorporated into the law by some stipulation or other. To be sure, I am not suggesting that every legal inference has to incorporate the facts it relies upon to be prefixed by an explicit statement to that effect; that usually happens when the legal classification of the relevant facts is controversial. Otherwise, the stipulation is mostly implicit or presupposed.[26] Notice, however, that even if the legal classification of the relevant facts is not contested or controversial, such classifications are always *contestable*. In principle, it is always possible to contest the incorporation of an alleged fact into the legal syllogism by claiming that, in the eyes of the relevant law, E [the action or event in the world] does not *count as* X [the fact as required by the law]. Either way, the stipulation is constitutive. In other words, whenever we have a legal argument of the form:

(a) According to the law in *S* (at time *t*, etc.) {if X [fact] then Y [legal result]}.
(b) X.
(c) According to the law in *S*, {Y}.

The minor premise, (b), is also prefixed. Typically, we just assume that to be the case; we normally take it for granted in the relevant conversational context. But the presupposition is essential. In other words, the complete inference here has another premise, often hidden (viz., presupposed), that the act or event in the world (un-prefixed) *counts as X*, legally speaking. Thus the complete inference looks like this:

(a) According to the law in *S* (at time *t*, etc.) {if X [fact] then Y [legal result]}.
(b1) E [something that happened in the world].

climbed a rope to kill its victim. As it happens, the Russell's viper is not a constrictor and cannot climb ropes. Does it matter? Is this the kind of fact that readers of Holmes mysteries are supposed to know? Also, note that the extent to which unstated facts are incorporated in fiction by implication is partly genre-dependent. Some fictional genres, such as realistic novels or detective stories, etc., are such that they tend to be rather generous with implicit incorporation of unstated facts, while other genres, such as surreal fiction, are probably less so.

[26] Lawyers often talk about this issue in terms of "finding of facts"; they recognize that legal inferences have to rely on a legal finding of facts—that is, facts legally established for the purposes of the relevant inference. However, this notion of an authoritative finding of fact is ambiguous between the finding that something actually happened in the world and the finding that it conforms to the relevant legal categorization of it. My discussion in the text concerns the latter issue.

(b2) According to the law in *S*, E counts as X, therefore, X.
(c) According to the law in *S*, {Y}.

An objection comes to mind here. Consider the case of John using his mobile phone while driving. One is very tempted to say that, given the legal requirement of (6*), John committed a misdemeanor, whether or not it is authoritatively determined that he did. After all, we want to say that he committed the offense even if he is never caught; he violated the law. Quite right. Nothing in what I suggest here, however, prevents us from alleging that John committed an offense even if he is never caught. The only point to bear in mind is that, when we make such a claim, we presuppose that the minor premise is incorporated into the legal context—that is, we presuppose that, in the eyes of the law, or, from a legal point of view, he used a mobile phone while driving (and thus has committed an offense). However, we must bear in mind that the presupposition is always in principle contestable; there is always the possibility of a legal claim to be made that John's conduct, whatever it was, does not count as X in the eyes of the law.[27] In other words, the inference from (6*) and the relevant facts entail (8*) only if (7*) is legally stipulated—that is, incorporated within the prefixed context. Not unlike in fiction, saying so in the law makes it so. Having seen that legal prescriptions are a type of exhortatives, this is not all that surprising.

[27] Suppose, e.g., that John talked on his mobile phone using the phone's built-in speaker, thus not holding it up to his ear, or suppose that John's passenger was holding up the phone to his ear; surely he can contest the stipulation of the minor premise here, arguing that what he did does not count as violating the law. And a court may need to decide on that.

4

Varieties of Vagueness in the Law

At the conclusion of chapter 1, we saw that a great deal of the asserted content of statutory law is semantically (and syntactically) encoded content. One of the main constraints on how much determinate content can be semantically encoded is due to the ubiquitous vagueness of expressions in a natural language. Vagueness in the law, however, as elsewhere, comes in different forms. Some of it is unavoidable, while other cases are optional and deliberately chosen by lawmakers. My main purpose in this chapter is to distinguish between different types of vagueness in the legal context and to explain their rationales. The argument proceeds in two main stages. The first part is taxonomical, mostly about the semantics of vagueness, and related linguistic indeterminacies, that we find in statutory language. The second part takes up each one of these different types of vagueness in law, suggesting some ways in which legal decision-makers reason with vague language, and some of the normative considerations that apply, depending on the kind of vagueness involved.

1. Varieties of Vagueness

In philosophy of language, the term "vagueness" is used to designate a particular aspect of the relation between the words we use in a natural language and the objects picked out, or designated, by those words. Consider, for example, a word like "rich" applied to persons. Some people in the world are clearly and undoubtedly rich. The set of people who satisfy this condition, that they are undoubtedly rich, we call the *definite extension* of the word. Innumerable other people are clearly and undoubtedly poor, not rich; we call this set the *definite nonextension* of the word. And then there are many borderline cases: these are people about whom, knowing all the relevant facts, there is no saying whether they are rich or not. From a semantic perspective, it would not be a mistake to say that "this person is rich," nor would it be a mistake to deny it, and say that "this person is not really, or not quite, rich." There is no answer—or, according to some views, there is an answer but it is not knowable[1]—to the question of whether a borderline case of "rich" is within the extension of the word or its nonextension.

Now, consider a particular person who is clearly and undoubtedly rich, if anyone is. Then imagine that we subtract one cent from his possessions. Surely he is still just as rich. Now subtract another cent, and he is still, undoubtedly, rich. But, of course, if we continue this subtraction, at some point we would have to doubt that the person is rich; the problem is that we cannot tell what that point is. There is no saying where exactly the borderline cases begin and where they end. This fuzziness of borderline cases is what gives rise to the famous sorites paradox.[2] We start with a true generalization, say, "Any person who has $100 million is rich." We add another true premise (called the "induction step"), saying, "If X is rich then X minus one cent is rich." Now the problem is that repeated applications of the induction step lead to a false conclusion. If you repeat the induction step many millions of times, your conclusion would have to be that a person who has very few dollars, or none at all, is rich, which is clearly false. And the problem, of course, is that we cannot tell where the induction step needs to be halted. There is no clear cutoff point in this

[1] According to the epistemic theory of vagueness (mostly developed by T. Williamson, *Vagueness*), there is a fact of the matter about the application of vague terms to what seems like borderline cases, but those facts are *not knowable*. The epistemic theory of vagueness is rather controversial, and, in any case, I will not explore its possible implications in this chapter. Mostly, it probably makes no difference, in the legal context, which particular theory of vagueness one works with. Scott Soames ("Vagueness and the Law") argues, however, that the ways in which we think about vagueness in the legal case may actually provide support to non-epistemic theories.

[2] What I call "fuzziness" of borderline cases is often called "second-order vagueness," meaning vagueness about where borderline cases begin and where they end. As long as it is clear that there is no first-order vagueness without second-order vagueness, the terminology should not be problematic. Still, I prefer to avoid the notion of second-order vagueness because I doubt that this is a matter of hierarchy.

(so-called) sorites sequence; there is no particular phase at which we can say that X is still rich but X minus one cent is no longer rich.[3]

Lawmakers do not tend to use such obviously vague terms as "rich" (or "tall," "bald," etc.). If Congress wanted to impose higher taxes on rich people, for example, it would define the regulation much more precisely, using income figures in dollar terms.[4] And, of course, the law can pick different figures for different purposes. But that does not mean that the law can avoid linguistic vagueness even when it has precise alternatives. Suppose that a law purports to impose a higher level of income tax on rich people, and defines the higher tax bracket in terms of a precise dollar figure of annual income, say, at a million dollars. This would be a very precise definition, but then we might face borderline cases about what counts as "income" (e.g., a gift from a relative, even a very small one? etc.). Even if "income" is defined by the relevant statute, the definition must use other words that are bound to have borderline cases. In short, the ordinary linguistic vagueness of general terms in a natural language cannot be avoided, thought its scope can be reduced in specific contexts.

Words like "rich," "mature," or "bald" are obviously and transparently vague. Other words are vague in exactly the same manner, but perhaps less obviously so. Consider, for example, a term like "entering" the premises, which forms part of the definition of burglary. Suppose that the defendant broke the window and had his arm through the boundary of the premises in question: did he enter the building? And what if only his finger got through? Or only some instrument he was using to break the window?[5] Let me call these *ordinary* cases of vagueness, as opposed to words or expressions that are obviously or transparently vague, such as "rich" or "mature," etc. Now you might think that obviousness (or transparency) is a vague criterion. That is true, of course, but, in the legal case, there is a certain significance to

[3] Notably, the epistemic theories of vagueness (and some others) deny the truth of the induction step. The main motivation behind the epistemic theories, and some other theories offered in the literature, is precisely the idea that we have to avoid the sorites paradox, otherwise we face serious problems with the principle of bivalence and the law of excluded middle in propositional logic. There is certainly no consensus in the literature about how deep the sorites paradox is, and whether it is avoidable. I intend to take no stance on this complex issue.

[4] There are exceptions, of course. For example, in child-support law in the U.S., some federal guidelines, adopted by most states, provide an exemption to payors who have "an extraordinarily high income." I will discuss this case later on.

[5] See, for example: *Commonwealth v. Cotto*, 52 Mass.App.Ct 225, 752 N.E.2d 768 (2001).

the transparency of vagueness in that the law typically tries to avoid it. We have countless laws using words such as "entering" or "premises," but very rarely laws using words such as "rich" or "mature." And it is an interesting question, I think, why that would be the case. After all, as we just saw, most general words we use in a natural language are vague, even if they do not carry their vagueness on their face. So why is it the case that the law strives to avoid one but not the other? Is it simply because some words like "mature" or "rich" are somehow vaguer than others, or just too obviously vague? Here is a reason to suspect that this is not the only, or even the main, reason: the law does not shy away from using words that seem to be obviously very vague, even extravagantly so (to borrow a term coined by Endicott[6]), such as "reasonable care," "due process," "neglect," "unconscionable," etc. So why is it that we rarely, if ever, find legal norms using words such as "rich" or "mature," but we find countless legal norms that employ terms such as "reasonable" or "neglect"?

The answer resides in a very important difference between words that are *transparently* vague and those we are calling *extravagantly* vague. The essential feature of vagueness, in the strict semantic sense, consists in the fact that when a word, W, is vague, there are bound to be borderline cases of W's application to objects that are in a space between W's definite extension and definite nonextension, objects about which there is no saying whether W applies or not. In other words, if W is vague then we are bound to have a sorites sequence.[7] This is clearly the case with words such as "rich," "mature," "bald," etc. However, in the kind of cases Endicott calls "extravagant" vagueness, the main semantic feature is neither the obviousness nor the extent of a sorites sequence in the application of the word to concrete cases, though both would also be present, of course.

To see this, let's work with the example that Endicott uses, of a UK statute making it an offense to cause a child to be "*neglected*...in a manner likely to cause him unnecessary suffering or injury to health." The word neglect is, indeed, extravagantly vague. But it does not seem to be any vaguer, so to speak, than "rich" or "mature"; it is not the case that we have more borderline cases here relative to the

[6] See T. Endicott, "The Value of Vagueness" at 24–25.

[7] I am not suggesting that this is the only semantic feature of words we can call vague in some sense, or that there is a consensus in the philosophical literature about what vagueness really is. It is at least one standard sense of vagueness and that is how I use the term here.

definite extension of the word. The main feature of extravagantly vague terms consists in the fact that they designate a *multidimensional* evaluation with (at least some) *incommensurable* constitutive elements. Neglecting a child is a very complex evaluative term. Many potential elements determine whether a certain case constitutes neglect. And, crucially, no common denominator would allow a quantitative comparison of the various constitutive elements on a single evaluative scale. We can say, for example, that leaving a child unattended for five hours is worse than leaving the same child unattended for two hours; or that it is worse to leave a two-year-old unattended for an hour than to leave a six-year-old unattended for the same amount of time. But even these two simple factors (age and time) are not quite commensurable: can we say whether it is worse to leave a two-year-old child unattended for ten minutes than a six-year-old unattended for two hours? And, of course, when you add more elements to the picture, such as the exact conditions in which the child is left unattended, the relevant environment, the child's level of maturity, and the like, problems of incommensurability become obvious.[8] Needless to say, this does not mean that we are unlikely to face borderline cases. Extravagantly vague terms are also vague in the ordinary sense of vagueness. But it is the multidimensionality of such terms that makes them particularly problematic and particularly resistant to precisification.

The difference between ordinary vagueness, transparent or not, and extravagant vagueness might be a matter of degree. Even the simplest vague terms, such as "bald" or "mature," are not single-dimensional; baldness, for example, might be a matter of both the number and the distribution of hair on a person's scalp. The main difference is, however, that the various elements that constitute the relevant predicate in standard cases of vagueness are not deeply and unavoidably incommensurable. Or, if some of them are, it is not typical for the incommensurability to pose a serious practical problem in determining whether an object or thing falls within the definite extension of the word or not. And this has an important consequence that explains the difference in their occurrence in law: when we have an ordinary vague term, with a sorites sequence, it is typically possible to stipulate a certain cutoff point

[8] I assume here that incommensurability is a relation between two (or more) items such that it is not true that one item is better or worse than the other, nor is it true that they are on a par with each other, according to the relevant evaluative dimension.

in the sequence. Though such cutoff points are bound to be somewhat arbitrary, for the law to determine an arbitrarily chosen cutoff point is not an arbitrary decision. Consider familiar cases: we know, for example, that a certain level of maturity should be required for the exercise of certain rights, such as voting in elections. Maturity is a vague term, obviously susceptible to a sorites sequence. But the law tends to stipulate a fairly precise cutoff point, such as eighteen years old for voting. Needless to say, the exact figure of eighteen years is both arbitrary and somewhat rough for the purpose.[9] But it is not arbitrary, in the sense of not being supported by reasons, to have such a cutoff point. For various obvious reasons of fairness and efficiency, it makes a lot of sense.[10] Furthermore, the cost of precisification in such cases is very clear: any reasonable cutoff point that the law chooses is bound to have some over—and some under—inclusiveness. Some persons older than eighteen are not mature enough to vote, and some persons younger than eighteen are actually mature enough to vote. Over—and under—inclusiveness is always the cost involved in such precisification. And, normally, we weigh this cost against the benefits of having a precise cutoff point. But now think about extravagantly vague terms: here, the main problem is not the sorites sequence. The main problem in such cases is the incommensurability of the various elements constituting the multidimensional evaluation. And because the main problem is not the sorites sequence, such cases resist the stipulation of an arbitrary cutoff point. You just cannot stipulate that, say, leaving a child unattended for *n* hours would constitute neglect, even if you make *n* a variable relative to age. Countless other factors are in play, and they cannot be weighed with reasonable precision against hours of un-attendance, the child's age, etc. And this is why the law cannot sensibly replace extravagantly vague terms with some stipulated precisification.

The kind of vagueness discussed so far is *semantic vagueness*, because it concerns the relations between the meaning of words and the objects they apply to. Vagueness, however, is not confined to the semantic aspect of language use. Expressions can be vague in the information they provide relative to a conversational context, whether they

[9] By this roughness I mean that we know that age is not the only dimension determining maturity, but it is the dominant one, and making the cutoff point determined by this single criterion, though inaccurate and oversimplified, for sure, is not an obvious miss nor a gross misconception.

[10] T. Endicott in "The Value of Vagueness" provides a very elegant account of these considerations in greater detail.

employ semantically vague terms or not. Suppose, for example, that during a political campaign, candidate M declares: "I did not receive any contributions from X, not a single dollar!" This statement does not seem particularly vague. But suppose the context is such that there is some suspicion that X channeled funds to the candidate's coffers indirectly, financing various organizations that are known to support M. Relative to *this context*, M's statement might be rather vague. Or, suppose that in response to my friend's enquiries about a movie I saw last night, I express praise for one of the actors, going on and on about how well she performed her role. If my friend was interested in my opinion about whether she should go and see the movie, my answer was probably too vague.

Conversational vagueness, as I will label such cases, does not have to be deliberately evasive. Expressions can be vague relative to a conversational context for a host of potential reasons, whether the speaker is deliberately evasive or not. The essential point here is that an expression that is not semantically vague can be vague relative to a specific conversation with respect to the information it contributes to the conversation. Contributions to a conversation can be more or less relevant. Some are clearly relevant and advance the common purpose of the conversation, others are clearly irrelevant (or baffling, or conspicuously evasive, etc.), and then there are borderline cases in between. In short, the idea is that conversational vagueness is typically a function of the relevance of the speaker's contribution to the conversation in question. Relevance is a pragmatic aspect of speech, always relative to a specific conversation, its exact context, its normative framework, and various presuppositions taken for granted by the parties to the conversation. Borderline cases about relevance are, basically, what I call conversational vagueness.[11]

Notice that conversational vagueness is quite independent of semantic vagueness. Just as an expression can be conversationally vague in a given context without using vague terms, an expression can be precise even when it uses a vague term applied to a borderline case. Suppose, for example, that in responding to my wife's question, I say, "I wore the blue jacket." This may give my wife all the information she wanted to have, even if my jacket's color is actually a borderline case of blue (somewhere between very dark navy blue

[11] It is possible that other conversational maxims, such as the maxim of quantity, also have borderline cases that would generate conversational vagueness in a similar way.

and black). If I only have one such jacket (say, the only other one I have is light brown), then by saying "the blue jacket" my expression picks out a singular object, relative to the conversational context that is mutually known to me and my wife. Similarly, when referring to somebody in a conversation as "the tall guy," the speaker may well succeed in referring to a particular person, even if the person referred to is not particularly tall, for example, when the only other person one could have mentioned in the specific context is particularly short, and this is known to both parties to the conversation.[12]

2. Vagueness in the Legal Context

Vagueness in legal language can arise in many different contexts: in legislation or agency regulations, in constitutional documents, in judicial decisions, in private contracts and wills, etc. For simplicity's sake, I will focus on the context of statutory interpretation. Thus, the standard case I will consider here would be an act of legislation that contains some relevant expression that is, in one of the senses defined above, vague. Since the application of the law to particular cases crucially depends on what the law says, applying a legal prescription to a borderline case of a general term used in the relevant statute would seem to be a paradigmatic case of the problem of vagueness in the law.[13]

a. Ordinary vagueness

Let us begin with a case of ordinary vagueness, using H. L. A. Hart's famous example (slightly modified).[14] A city ordinance stipulates that "No motor vehicles are allowed in the park." Now, we know what motor vehicles are; the definite extension is pretty clear. But suppose that the question arises whether a bicycle powered by a small electric engine also counts as a "motor vehicle" for the purposes of this ordinance and thus is prohibited from entering the park. Can we say whether an electric bicycle is a motor vehicle or not? The answer would seem

[12] It is not essential to my point here that the examples in the text have something to do with the distinction between referential and attributive uses of definite descriptions; other kinds of examples will be used later.

[13] In chapter 6, we will discuss the role of general (and very vague) concepts, as opposed to conceptions, in constitutional documents.

[14] See H. L. A. Hart, "Positivism and the Separation of Law and Morals."

to be that from a semantic perspective it can go either way. It would not seem to be a mistake to say that it is, nor would it be a mistake to say that it is not.[15]

We saw earlier that semantically vague expressions are not necessarily vague about the information they convey in a particular conversational setting. Speakers can use a vague term, even if applied to a semantically borderline case, to convey information that is precise enough in the specific context of the conversation. Applied to the kind of cases we are discussing here, this means that, when a court faces a decision about the classification of a borderline case of a vague term, the semantic indeterminacy of the classification does not necessarily entail that the law says nothing about it. The context of the legislation, its overt purposes, and similar pragmatic factors may determine an answer in some concrete cases. Suppose, for example, that, in our case, the city ordinance was enacted in response to protests by residents about noise and pollution in the park. One can argue that such a context makes it clear that the ordinance was not intended to prohibit the use of vehicles that are neither noisy nor polluting, and hence it was not intended to prohibit electric bicycles.

In chapters 1 and 2, I cautioned against moving too swiftly from analysis of ordinary conversational settings to legal speech. In an ordinary conversation, the context is usually rich enough to enable hearers to grasp the content conveyed by the speaker, even when the content asserted is somewhat different from the meaning of the words/sentences that the speaker uttered. In the legal case, however, context is often not rich enough to justify such inferences with a great deal of certainty. Perhaps the ordinance about vehicles in the park was initially motivated by the neighbors' protests about noise and pollution; perhaps it was enacted in response to such demands. But this would not necessarily entail that reducing noise and pollution are the exclusive purposes of the ordinance. Legislatures often use a particular social-political context to motivate an act of legislation, but then enact it with broader purposes, aiming to solve other problems in its vicinity as well. Truth be told, it is very difficult to generalize.

[15] Furthermore, it is easy to see how we get a sorites sequence here: suppose we say that an electric bicycle is not a motor vehicle. Then what about a small golf cart powered by an electric engine? A golf cart powered by a regular engine? A small scooter? And so on and so forth. As I explain in the text below, however, sorites sequences, which result from semantic features of words used, should not be confused with slippery-slope arguments, particularly of the causal–predictive type.

Sometimes the context of an act of legislation is clear enough to warrant conclusions about its assertive content, even if the particular case is semantically borderline. A nice case in point is *Garner v. Burr*: the British Road Traffic Act of 1930 stipulated that any "vehicle" traveling on a public highway must be fitted with pneumatic tires. Mr. Burr fitted a poultry shed with iron wheels and pulled it with his tractor on a stretch of a highway. The court of appeals reasoned, quite sensibly, that even if a poultry shed fitted on wheels is not quite a vehicle, it counts as a vehicle for the purposes of the law, because the manifest purpose of the law requiring pneumatic tires is simply to prevent damage to the asphalt roads.[16]

Quite often, however, the context is just not sufficiently clear or determinate to justify such conclusions. And then, of course, semantically borderline cases remain genuine borderline cases, so to speak, and the court would need to make a reasoned decision about which way to classify the borderline case, given all the normative considerations that bear on it. Such decisions would not be an instance of applying the law but of extending it or narrowing it—that is, adding a precisification that goes beyond what the statute actually asserts. And, of course, courts often do just that.

One might be tempted to think that, at least in criminal cases, the rule of leniency might resolve the issue: if the definition of the criminal offense leaves some doubt about its application to the particular features of the conduct in question, as it clearly does when the conduct is a borderline case of the relevant definition of the offense, then the doubts must be resolved in favor of the defendant. But this is illusory. The rule of leniency may do the trick in cases of ambiguity, but not, generally speaking, in cases of vagueness. What makes vagueness semantically problematic is not simply the fact that there are borderline cases about the application of the vague term, but the fact that there is a great deal of fuzziness about where those borderline cases begin and where they end. Consider, for example, the case of burglary we mentioned earlier; suppose that you regard someone who broke the window and only got his tool through the border of the premises in question as a borderline case of entering the premises, and, thus, true to the rule of leniency, you would decide to acquit the defendant. Now

[16] *Garner v. Burr* (1951), 1KB 31. The case is discussed by Endicott in his entry on "Law and Language" in the *Stanford Encyclopedia of Philosophy* and by R. A. Cartson in "Legal Texts and Canons of Construction" at 20–21.

another defendant comes along who had his finger through the premises, and you apply the rule of leniency here as well and acquit. And then the next one comes along who had his whole arm through the window, and then one who had half of his body through the window, and so on and so forth. Where exactly would you stop applying the rule of leniency? In short, it is an essential aspect of vagueness that we have no clear demarcation of where borderline cases begin and where they end. The rule of leniency, even if you interpret it very broadly, just cannot solve such issues; it cannot determine its own application when its application is in doubt. The rule of leniency is applicable and helpful when the linguistic indeterminacy is due to ambiguity, not vagueness. If the definition of a criminal offense is plausibly ambiguous, lexically or syntactically, then the rule of leniency can apply, requiring disambiguation in favor of the defendant.[17]

It is, I think, quite impossible to suggest general guidelines about how courts should go about making such precisification in borderline cases; the considerations that bear on particular cases are enormously varied. But it is easy to say what kind of reasoning courts should avoid. They should avoid relying on the sorites paradox as a way of making a (type of) slippery-slope argument.

A sorites slippery-slope argument takes the following worry as an argument against the inclusion of a borderline case under a vague term: let us say that the relevant expression is W, the definite extension of W is o_n, and let us assume that the court is asked to determine whether o_{n+1} is W or not. Now suppose the court reasons that o_{n+1} is W because it is very similar to o_n; it has almost all of the features that make an o W, just ever so slightly less so. So now we will have a ruling that o_{n+1} should be included under W. Then the next case might come along, o_{n+1+1}, which is very similar to o_{n+1}, has almost all of the relevant features that make it W, just ever so slightly less so. Thus, a decision might be reached that o_{n+1+1} is also W. And then the next case comes along... until we are bound to reach the conclusion that o_{n+m} is also W, when clearly it is not. Therefore, the argument concludes, it would be a mistake to make the first step. Better not to decide that o_{n+1} is W from the start.[18]

[17] Ambiguity will be discussed in chapter 5.

[18] See, for example, *Randall v. Orange County Council*, 17 Cal.4th 736, 952 P.2d 261, concerning the question of whether the Boy Scouts of America counts as a "business establishment" for the purposes of the California Unruh Civil Rights Act.

Why is this a bad argument? Because it can be applied with equal force to *any* borderline case of a vague term. As we saw earlier, we get paradoxical results whenever we have a sorites sequence. An argument based on paradox is never a good argument. In other words, whenever we have a sorites sequence, we can easily construct a type of slippery-slope argument because the whole point of the sorites sequence is that there is no semantically determined cutoff point; there is no particular point at which we can say that the sequence needs to be halted, that it can go no further. Thus, pointing out that there is a kind of sorites slippery slope here is just stating the semantic feature of vagueness; no conclusion should follow from it. Any classification of a borderline case is going to be arbitrary from a linguistic point of view. The relevant question is whether there are good reasons to stipulate a certain arbitrary cutoff point or not, and, if there are, what reasons would bear on the question of where the law should put it?

To be sure, suggesting that a sorites slippery slope is always a bad argument does not mean that no plausible versions of a slippery-slope argument can apply to such cases. A *causal–predictive* version of a slippery-slope argument may well be relevant. The worry in the causal version is that the cutoff point stipulated by the court's decision is too far removed from the definite extension so that actual, real-life factors may cause the legal consequences to slip too far down the road to undesirable results. Notice that the nature of such an argument is empirical and predictive: the worry is that if the court includes a given borderline case under a vague term, then future decision-makers, such as agencies, lower courts, or even the same court in future cases, might find it difficult to resist the temptation to go further down the road, reaching results that one finds objectionable. Now, this is a matter of prediction, and such arguments tend to be rather speculative. Though the concern is empirical in nature about matters of fact, it is not unrelated to the nature of vagueness. The concern that motivates causal slippery-slope arguments derives its force from the fuzziness of borderline cases, from the fact that there is no obvious or salient cutoff point that can warn us against slipping down the road too far from the original reasons that justified the legal rule in question.

Given the speculative nature of causal slippery-slope arguments, they should always be treated with great caution. The burden of proof should be high, because it is the nature of slippery-slope arguments that they counsel against doing something that would be the right decision on the merits of the case at hand, only due to a fear that future decisions are likely to lead us astray. Thus, at the very least, the argument should provide sufficient evidence that likely errors in the future will be difficult to avoid. Gut feelings and speculations, which are mostly what one finds in such cases, should not be enough.

b. Transparent vagueness

Transparently vague terms, such as "tall," "mature," "rich," etc., are rarely found in statutory language. But they are not entirely absent. In some cases, and typically in addition to a set of much more precise regulations, one finds that the law includes a transparently vague term as part of its regulatory scheme. Often the purpose of such vague additions to a regulatory scheme in a given area is preemptive: legislatures want to safeguard against the possibility that some unpredictable, yet clearly wrong (or otherwise relevant), conduct does not fall between the cracks of the set of precise rules that purports to govern the area in question. There is an endless variety of permutations; one just cannot predict them all.[19]

Be this as it may, the most obvious aspect of legislating transparently vague standards, whether in the kind of cases discussed above or others, is that the legislature in effect delegates the decision of how to make the standard more specific to the courts or to administrative agencies. Using vague legislative language is, actually, the main technique for legislatures to delegate power to the courts without explicitly saying that this is what they are doing. Accordingly, there are two main types of reasons for opting for such transparently vague regulation: sometimes the vague language is simply a result of a compromise between legislators enacting the bill. Legislators often have conflicting aims or intentions with respect to a bill they would want to enact, and if neither side can muster the requisite majority for their position, opposing sides may settle on wording that is sufficiently vague to let each party hope that their specific purposes might win the day in future decisions by the relevant courts or agencies that get

[19] Traffic regulations often have some kind of a requirement to drive with reasonable attention to the conditions of the road. There are also countless such examples in U.S. tax legislation. For instance, section 541 imposes an accumulated earnings tax on corporate-retained earnings beyond those retained "for the reasonable needs of the business." Section 535(c): tax-free mergers are typically conditioned on the transaction having a corporate "business purpose." Etc. etc.

to interpret the act in question. (Or, I presume, sometimes there is no such hope, only the attempt to conceal from the constituency that one gave up.)

Compromise, by its nature, is regarded by the parties to it as second best. The use of vagueness in the law, however, is not confined to such second-best choices. Sometimes there are good reasons to opt for a vague term in an act of legislation as a means of delegating the decision to the courts, and those are mostly the kind of cases I want to focus on. But let me answer an objection here before we proceed.

Some writers suggest that vaguely worded regulation in some areas is justified by the need to delegate the relevant decisions not to the courts but to the law's subjects, to those whose behavior the law purports to regulate. The idea is that, in some cases, instead of telling people what it is exactly that they ought to do (or not to do), it is better to set a vague standard, leaving it for the subjects themselves to exercise their own discretion and take responsibility for the choices they make. So when the law tells drivers that, no matter what, you ought to drive *carefully*, the law imposes on the drivers themselves the responsibility to determine what careful driving is under the circumstances. It is your responsibility, the law says to its subjects, to determine what is right or reasonable under the circumstances, and you need to bear the consequences of your own choices. And, some writers claim, this is sometimes a very good idea; it is as it should be.[20]

Presumably, the attractive feature of this rationale for vague regulation is that it respects people's autonomy or, at least, forces people to take responsibility for their decisions. Writers who like this idea admit that in some cases there might be a concern about chilling effect, but I think that they underestimate the normative problem here. Consider this example: my teenage daughter is going out on a Saturday night. I want to make sure that she gets back home at a reasonable hour, so I face a choice here: I can either tell her, "Make sure to be home no later than 2 a.m.," or I can be much vaguer, and tell her, "Make sure not to come home too late!" Now, we might think that the vague instruction is more respectful of my daughter's autonomy. It is more educational, in a sense, too, because it makes her more responsible for her own actions, which is generally a good attitude to foster. So far, so good. But now let us suppose that there is a sanction looming here—that is, suppose that my daughter knows that I am the one who gets to determine what

[20] J. Waldron, "Vagueness and the Guidance of Action"; T. Endicott, "The Value of Vagueness."

would count as "too late" to come home, and that if I decide that she came home too late, I get to impose a penalty. And let us further suppose that she cannot be sure, in fact she only has a vague sense of what I would consider "too late" under the circumstances. Notice that if my daughter knows exactly what I have in mind when I say "too late," then my instruction is no longer really vague. (More precisely, my instruction is still semantically vague, of course, but conversationally, pragmatically precise.) Now we might begin to doubt that the vague instruction is more conducive to her autonomy or more respectful of her dignity. In all likelihood, it might have a chilling effect. If the sanction is not trivial, she would need to play it safe and err on the side of caution, and the more threatening the sanction is, the greater the margin of safety she would need to allow.

The legal case is, of course, in line with the latter part of the example. When the law regulates conduct with vague standards, it puts the decision about sanctions for violation in the hands of the courts, and it is the court that gets to determine, ex post, whether the subject violated the standard or not. Therefore, the real effect of such vague regulation is transferring to the subjects not the kind of decision that is respectful of their autonomy or moral agency, but the burden of trying to predict what the courts will decide. And the less information they have about it, and/or the more severe the cost of violation, the more the subjects would need to err on the side of caution. Perhaps in some cases this legislative strategy is efficient or justified, but I do not quite see how, morally speaking, it is particularly respectful of the subjects' moral dignity or autonomy.[21]

None of this is meant to suggest that there are no cases in which there are good reasons to delegate the decision about precisification of vague standards to the courts. On the contrary, there are many such cases. But the rationale of delegation of power must be derived from considerations pertaining to the relative institutional competence of legislatures vis-à-vis the courts or other decision-making agencies.[22]

[21] In fact, the problem is often more severe, because a serious concern about fairness also comes into the picture. The vaguer a legal regulation is, in the sense discussed here, the more crucial it becomes for potential litigants to have information that enables them to predict courts' decisions, which gives repeat players, mostly large corporations, considerable advantage over ordinary citizens.

[22] It is important in this context to think about the law enforcement agents who need to make decisions on the ground, as it were; in various contexts, such as traffic regulation, for example, decisions have to be made by law enforcement agents on the spot, and then it is probably not a good idea to give those law enforcement agents too much discretion in determining whether the law has been violated or not.

That is the real choice here, not the concern for the subjects' autonomy. Furthermore, I will argue that there is typically a much stronger case for the legislature to delegate to the courts decisions about specifications of extravagantly vague terms than cases in which the legislature uses a transparently vague term. In any case, different kinds of reasons apply here.

What reasons, if any, might legislatures have for using a transparently vague term as a means of delegating the precisification of a vague standard to the courts? Remember that the main problem in such cases is to set a cutoff point in the sorites sequence. Is there any reason to think that the courts will do a better job in that? Generally speaking, probably not. The relatively infrequent use of transparently vague terms in legislation suggests that it is generally recognized that legislatures are better equipped to make those kind of decisions compared with the courts. Furthermore, it is worth keeping in mind that courts' decisions, which are based on particular cases adjudicated, inevitably have a retroactive effect; unlike legislative acts and guidelines issued in advance, the decision of a court applies to conduct that has already occurred and determines a resolution to the case ex post. So there is always some cost of retroactivity involved in judicial, as opposed to legislative, decisions.[23]

I want to suggest that there are certain cases where delegating to the courts the decision of determining the particular cutoff point in a sorites sequence makes a lot of sense—namely, when the following two conditions obtain: first, the precisification is particularly context-sensitive, and second, it is an area of conduct where the parties concerned do not have good reasons to know in advance the exact regulatory content that applies to them. Consider, for example, the law I mentioned earlier in a note, of granting exemption from the federal guidelines concerning child support on the basis of "extraordinarily high income." Why not have the legislature stipulate a certain income figure as a cutoff point? The answer is twofold. First, the relevant considerations are very context sensitive. The rationale of the exemption has something to do with the fact that the needs of children are not unlimited, that there is no reason to allow either the

[23] In some areas, precisification requires a great deal of expertise, of the kind that legislatures typically lack. But in such cases, legislatures tend to delegate the decisions to administrative agencies, not so much to the courts. And administrative agencies tend to issue detailed general guidelines, not case-by-case decisions.

children or the custodial parent to have an extravagant lifestyle. But, of course, these things tend to vary a great deal with particular circumstances. The difference between comfort and luxury profoundly depends on the environment in which one lives, the kind of opportunities available to others in one's vicinity, etc. Therefore, it makes a lot of sense to avoid a generally stipulated cutoff point and allow the courts to set it on a case-by-case basis.

Second, there is a distinction between the kind of regulations where it is important for the law's subjects to know, ex ante, what the law requires, and those cases in which prior knowledge of the exact legal regulation is not very important. In most cases, when we plan our conduct in a given area, knowing what the law requires or permits is of crucial importance. But not in all cases. And child support belongs to the latter. Parents do not (and certainly should not) plan separation or divorce from their spouse on the basis of considerations about the exact amount of child support they will be required to pay. Ex post determination of such matters does not frustrate legitimate expectations, as long as those determinations are within reason, of course.[24] Thus, allowing the courts to determine, on a case-by-case basis, the exact cutoff point in a sorites sequence—which would normally have a retroactive, ex post facto element—is not normatively problematic in such cases. Notice, however, that when the rationale of opting for transparently vague terms consists in the particular context sensitivity of the relevant factors, decisions made by the courts on a case-by-case basis should have very limited precedential effect. If the whole point of letting the courts decide such matters derives from the inherent difficulties involved in ex ante generalizations, then granting courts' decisions too much precedential effect would defeat the rationale of the delegation of power to the courts.

c. *Extravagant vagueness*

It may seem paradoxical that legislatures have much stronger reasons to delegate decisions to the courts when the relevant concept in play is extravagantly vague. But that is actually the case, and the ubiquity of such terms in legislation might attest to the fact. Let me explain

[24] This idea is supported by the fact that most U.S. states do not allow child-support arrangements to form part of a prenuptial agreement. U.S. tax legislation, as I mentioned earlier, is also replete with transparently vague terms. It is not all that surprising, given the fact that, in U.S. federal tax law, quite generally, retroactivity is not regarded as a major concern.

why this is so. Remember that the main feature of extravagantly vague terms consists in their multidimensional aspect, not so much in the sorites sequence they entail. Thus, it might help if we focus our attention on the ways in which we make choices or decisions in cases involving multidimensional and incommensurable elements. Suppose, for example, that one of your colleagues received an offer to move to a different job in a different city, and she needs to make up her mind about whether to accept it. So let us assume that this is what she knows: the new job pays better, but it will involve a bit more teaching; she will be able to afford better housing, though the commute will be a bit longer; and the faculty in the new place is probably stronger than in her current department, but the quality of the graduate students is not as high. And then there is the fact that she will need to move from a small college town to a big city, with all the differences involved in that. And so on and so forth.

The essential point is that the various factors that your colleague needs to consider present her with a problem of incommensurability. It is very difficult to decide, on rational grounds, how much better the housing has to be relative to a given addition of commute time, and even more difficult to think about how to compare, say, better housing with more teaching or lower quality of students. So how can one make a rational decision in such cases? There seem to be two main possibilities here: in some cases, a particular factor stands out as more or less decisive. Your colleague may think, for example, that improving her housing condition is much more important to her than other considerations in play, and then she would assign it a much greater weight in her deliberation. And this may well tilt the balance in favor of a particular decision. However, if no such decisive factor is in play, her only choice is to make an all-things-considered holistic judgment here; she would need to take everything she deems relevant to the choice into account and decide between the two packages, as it were, in a holistic manner. She would look at the whole thing, so to speak, and ask herself which one seems more attractive, overall. There is no guarantee, of course, that such a holistic method would yield a reasoned preference for one of the options, but then she might as well just flip a coin.

Now consider the example we used earlier, of an extravagantly vague legal norm such as "neglecting a child." Suppose you are presented with the particular facts of a given case that would seem to be a case of neglect. Like in the job-offer example, it is quite possible that a particular fact of the case stands out as more or less decisive.

Upon hearing that the care provider left a baby in a bathtub full of water unattended for half an hour, you may not need to hear much more. But, of course, many cases are not like that. In many actual cases, there is not any particular conduct that decisively counts as neglect, but the overall behavior of the care provider, over time and in varying circumstances, might well amount to criminal neglect. And you can only make this kind of judgment holistically, looking at the whole package, so to speak. And again, the whole package may not give you a decisive answer; borderline cases cannot be ruled out.[25]

I hope we can see the reason for trying to avoid ex ante specifications of how to resolve such issues. Just as it would make very little sense to decide in advance how you would react to any job offer you might receive in the indefinite future, or to try to make yourself a list of specific conditions that such an offer would have to meet (and to what extent) for you to accept it, it makes little sense for the law to try to legislate in any great detail what counts as neglecting a child. Even if one can think in advance of some factors that may stand out as decisive, often there are no such decisive factors in play, only all-things-considered, holistic judgments to make. And, of course, if these kinds of decisions cannot be made ex ante, legislatures have no choice but to delegate the decisions to the courts on a case-by-case basis. And here too, for reasons we mentioned earlier, it would be a mistake to assign courts' decisions in particular cases great precedential value. The whole point of delegating such decisions to the courts is that they have to be made ex post, on the basis of the particular features of the case at hand.

Some of the more familiar examples of extravagantly vague terms in law are a bit more complex than that, because they tend to be partially defined. Consider, for example, the use of the word "corruption" in the context of bribery laws: the definition of bribery under federal law (18 USC 201) defines bribery as "*corruptly* giving, offering or promising anything of value to a public official or candidate to influence any official act." The word "corruption" is, no doubt, extravagantly vague. Very much like "neglect," in most cases

[25] In some rare cases in the U.S., vague statutory references to a child's "welfare" or a child's "neglect" have been struck down as unconstitutionally vague. See, for example, *Roe v. Conn*, 417 F. Supp. 769 (1976). Most of these cases, as *Roe v. Conn* exemplifies, are entangled with problems of racial discrimination and racial bias at the enforcement level, and I am told by experts that these kind of issues are almost always lurking in the background of void for vagueness constitutional cases.

the determination of whether a given set of circumstances amounts to corruption has to be made contextually and holistically. But the law does not quite leave it at that. Corruption is partly defined by various rule-like decisions, such as requiring some quid pro quo element, whereby merely gaining access to officials does not count as corrupt. So we end up here with a tension between two kinds of reasoning: on the one hand, we have the extravagantly vague term, aiming to allow the courts to form a holistic, all-things-considered judgment of the particular case at hand; on the other hand, we have some specific rules that aim to shape such decisions and determine, in advance, *some of the conditions* that the relevant conduct has to meet to count as corrupt. This compromise between different types of legal regulation, embodied in the partial definition of a transparently vague term such as corruption, reflects the fact that the law needs to set some fairly specific guidelines in advance, but that there is a limit to how specific those guidelines should be. The limit, however, is not epistemic; it does not derive from lack of knowledge or limited foresight. It derives from the multidimensionality of the evaluative elements that constitute the idea of corruption. And, of course, corruption is just one example. Similar considerations apply to legal concepts such as "due process," considerations of "equity," protection of "privacy," and many others. I venture to speculate that most extravagantly vague terms deployed in the law are partially defined.

d. Conversational vagueness

I want to conclude this discussion with the opposite type of case, where we have a legal formulation that is semantically precise relative to a certain object or instance of application, but conversationally vague in the context of its utterance. To illustrate the (very limited) point that I want to make here, consider the case of *FDA v. Brown & Williamson Tobacco Corp.*[26] The question in this case was whether the FDA was granted the authority to regulate tobacco products. The relevant part of the statute defining the FDA's authority to regulate drugs said that the FDA has the authority to regulate "articles (other than food) intended to affect the structure or any function of the body." Now, if you think about it from a semantic perspective, surely you

[26] 529 U.S. 120 (2000). I am certainly not suggesting that this is the only issue that is central to this complicated case, nor that it bears on the desirable result.

would think that cigarettes and other tobacco products are intended to do just that, "affect the . . . function of the body," and hence they are clearly within the *definite extension* of the relevant expression here. So why is this regulation conversationally vague in the context? The answer, which gave rise to this famous litigation, consists in the combination of two additional facts. First, the legal fact that if tobacco falls under the jurisdiction of the FDA, other parts of the statute render it clear that the FDA must prohibit its sale. Second, the fact that between the enactment of the law in 1965 and the time of the court's decision in 2000, Congress enacted six separate pieces of legislation regulating the sale, advertisement, etc., of tobacco products, clearly presupposing that the general sale of tobacco products is perfectly legal. Thus, the conflict between different pieces of legislation here, and their accompanying presuppositions, renders it questionable whether tobacco products fall within the ambit of the authority granted to the FDA. In the overall context of tobacco regulation, the relevant statutory expression is conversationally vague, even if it is not an instance of a semantically borderline case.[27]

There is, I think, an interesting lesson here: contextual knowledge is often deemed helpful in determining some asserted content that would otherwise be under-determined or vague. Sometimes, however, the opposite is the case; an expression that is not particularly vague or indeterminate becomes pragmatically or conversationally vague precisely because the particular context of the conversation makes it doubtful that the expression applies to its ordinary semantic extension. Given the complex contextual background of legal regulations, I suspect that conversational vagueness in law is much more common than one might have thought. Sometimes context makes thing less, rather than more, clear.

[27] In one clear sense, this is an oversimplification because I ignore the legal significance of the time sequence between the different pieces of legislation. But my point in the text is not to analyze the case, only to illustrate a general point.

5

Textualism in Context

Textualism deserves special attention in any linguistic analysis of statutory law because it purports to be based on it. As a theory of statutory interpretation, it urges judges to interpret the law according to what the legislature has actually communicated in its enacted law, eschewing any reliance on legislative intent or legislative purposes. I agree with John Manning that it is difficult to get a sense of what textualism is all about without paying attention to the ways in which it forms a critique of intentionalism and purposivism, and aims to replace them.[1] Manning is a textualist and I am not. My aim in this chapter is to show why nobody should be—which is not to deny that textualism brings some important insights to the debate over statutory interpretation. It certainly does, and some of them need to be taken seriously. However, those sound insights do not lead to the conclusions textualists argue for, and, as a whole, textualism is not nearly as helpful a theory of statutory interpretation as its proponents claim.

A theory of statutory interpretation aims to answer the question of how judges should go about trying to resolve an interpretative question they encounter about statutory law. But, of course, a lot depends here on the question of how the notion of interpretation is understood. A number of legal philosophers have argued (or assumed) that some process of interpretation mediates *any* application of a legal directive to a concrete factual situation or a concrete legal result. According to this view, called interpretivism, each and every understanding of what the law requires in a given situation is a result of some interpretation

[1] J. F. Manning, "What Divides Textualists from Purposivists?"

or other. I have long rejected this view and argued that we should see interpretation as an exception to the standard and ordinary understanding of what the law says. The need for interpretation only arises when something is not quite clear, when there is some plausible question about how to understand what the law requires.

Since I have argued against interpretivism elsewhere at length, there is no need to repeat those arguments here.[2] Let me try, however, to explain the motivation for holding a narrow sense of interpretation in the context of our discussion here. The main point is that, when the assertive content of a legal directive is not in any plausible doubt, hearers do not resort to interpretation in figuring out the content asserted. It is true, as we saw in chapter 1, that assertive content is often pragmatically enriched content, going beyond the semantic content of the relevant expression. The hearer's ability to grasp the pragmatically enriched content involves a defeasible *inference* from the semantic content of the expression used, the contextual background that is common knowledge between speaker and hearer, and the relevant normative framework governing the conversation in question. Now, of course, we can call this inferential process *interpretation* if we like. And then we could say that, in most cases of ordinary conversations, hearers need to interpret the utterance in the context of its expression in order to grasp what is said. But this process of interpretation, if you want to call it by that name, does not carry with it any of the evaluative considerations usually associated with genuine cases of interpretation. By "genuine" cases, I mean those in which interpretation involves the exercise of some judgment, when it calls for some evaluative considerations about what would make more sense, what would fit better, or what would be a better understanding of the object of interpretation compared to other plausible interpretations of it. It is one of the hallmarks of the idea of interpretation that if there is one plausible interpretation of X, there might be other, different interpretations of X, which would also be warranted or sensible. Interpretation, in other words, is called for when a given understanding of an expression or some other object bearing some meaning is in some doubt and a case can be made to prefer one understanding over another.

Therefore, a genuine case of statutory interpretation arises, I will assume here, in two main types of cases: (i) when there is some plausible doubt about what the legislature actually said or implicated; or

[2] See my *Interpretation and Legal Theory* (revised 2nd ed.) and *Philosophy of Law*, chs. 4 and 6.

(ii) when the communication intention of a legal directive is clear enough, but there is some plausible doubt about how the content of the directive bears on the particular question or problem that needs to be resolved. Now, if you doubt that these two types of cases form only an exception, think about the countless legal disputes—by far the most, actually—that never make it to the courts. And then keep in mind that legal cases adjudicated in lower courts often concern factual disputes. The proportion of cases where there is a plausible disagreement about the applicable law, which are the cases that tend to reach appellate courts, is very small; the vast majority of legal disputes do not reach appellate courts simply because the law is clear enough, and nobody wants to waste costly resources on hopeless litigation.

Statutory interpretation is called for when there is some plausible doubt about what the law says or about how what it does say would settle the case at hand. As such, statutory interpretation must be guided by some views about the role of the judiciary vis-à-vis the legislature in their respective authorities to shape the law and to modify it when circumstances call for completions and modifications. Justice Scalia is very clear about this point when he says that "it is simply incompatible with democratic government, or indeed, even with fair government, to have the meaning of a law determined by what the lawgiver meant, rather than by what the lawgiver promulgated."[3] Two ideas are suggested in this statement. The first, which is quite sound, is that the starting point for a theory of statutory interpretation is normative, mostly about the appropriate allocation of power between the legislature and the judiciary in a democratic or, generally, a fair regime. However, there is also a second suggestion here—namely, that we face a choice between two options: either try to figure out what the lawgiver meant, or else comply with what the lawgiver promulgated. This is a spurious choice, I will argue. In most cases, and certainly in most cases that matter, there is no such interpretative choice to make.

The argument of this chapter proceeds in three stages. First, I will briefly outline what textualism is in light of its critique of purposivism and intentionalism. Second, I will try to explain the view of language and communication that is required to make sense of textualism, arguing that, at its core, textualism actually assumes a very sensible view of what is said by the law. In the third part, however, I will try

[3] A. Scalia, *A Matter of Interpretation*, 17.

to show why those same ideas about linguistic communication render textualism rather unhelpful as a theory of statutory interpretation.

1. Textualism as Opposed to What?

a. Intentionalism

It might be helpful to begin with a brief outline of the two main theories of statutory interpretation prevalent in U.S. federal courts that textualism strives to replace—namely, intentionalism and purposivism. According to intentionalism, when judges face an interpretative question about statutory law, they should, first and foremost, strive to ascertain the actual intention of the legislature that bears on the issue at hand, and, if they manage to find out what that intention was, they must defer to it and decide the case accordingly. For example, suppose that a law makes it illegal to engage in certain forms of discrimination in the workplace, with various legal consequences attached to discriminatory practices. Let us assume that the statute stipulates a partial definition of what counts as "wrongful discrimination" for the purposes of this statute but leaves it unclear whether an act would count as wrongful discrimination only if it was intended as discriminatory or wrongful, even if the relevant agent had no intention to discriminate. Now, it is not difficult to imagine various scenarios in which legislators who enacted the bill would have had certain views about this question. Perhaps they by and large assumed that discrimination is wrongful only if it is intentional, or, vice versa, that it does not have to be intentional. And it is not difficult to imagine scenarios in which the available information about the legislative history of the statute would reveal that one of these options reflects the intentions of most legislators, or perhaps the intentions of those legislators who drafted the bill and played key roles in its enactment, with others acquiescing and going along with the relevant conception. Intentionalism urges judges to take this kind of legislative history very seriously. It urges judges to try to figure out the actual intentions and purposes that guided the relevant piece of legislation, striving to extrapolate an answer from those intentions and purposes to the question they face.

No serious intentionalist would argue that there is always some relevant legislative intention to discover (that is, over and above the communication intention to enact the legal content asserted by the statutory provision, of course). Sometimes, no doubt, knowing all the relevant legislative history, the only plausible conclusion is that the legislature had no intentions or purposes or any other thoughts that bear on the interpretative issue either way. (We discussed a possible scenario of this in chapter 4.) The point that intentionalists make, however, is that when a particular legislative intention is ascertainable to a reasonable degree, judges should comply with it—that is, decide the case in a way that effectuates the relevant legislative intent.

There are three main and well-known objections to intentionalism, and textualists tend to flag those concerns. First, and perhaps foremost, is the normative question of why legislative intentions should matter at all. Why would it be legally relevant that the legislature intended to achieve X or promote Y in enacting a law if that intention is not expressed in what the law says? (Call this the *principled objection*.) Second, many doubt that judges can figure out what the legislative intentions really were. In fact, some argue that the tools available for courts to inquire into legislative intent are such that the relevant material is bound to yield skewed and biased results, mostly favoring the vocal supporters of a law who use strategic maneuvers to overemphasize their legislative agenda over the views of the median legislators who formed the majority.[4] (Call this the *reliability objection*.) Finally, there are those who raise concerns about the conceptual possibility of attributing intentions to a large and diverse group of people such as a legislature. (Call this the *conceptual objection*.)

This is not the place to elaborate on these concerns and assess their plausibility. I will confine myself here to a few remarks. First, textualism would be ill advised to make too much of the conceptual objection. If you doubt that it is possible to attribute some collective intentions to the legislature as a whole, you will get into trouble when you claim that judges should take very seriously what the law communicates as opposed to what you might think that the law aimed to achieve. As we saw in chapter 1, communication by legislation is a speech act and, like any other complex act, it is done intentionally. If legislatures cannot act with a collective intention, then enactment cannot be a speech act either. In other words, if you take the communicative aspect of lawmaking seriously, as textualism clearly does, you must allow for the

[4] See, for example, A. Vermeule, *Judging Under Uncertainty: An Institutional Theory of Legal Interpretation*; D. B. Rodriguez and B. R. Weingast, "The Positive Political Theory of Legislative History: New Perspectives on the 1964 Civil Rights Act and Its Interpretation."

possibility of collective intentionality, simply because legislation, on this view, must be viewed as a form of a collective speech act.

Indeed, I do not think that this point has entirely escaped textualists' attention. Most of the skepticism they raise about intentionalism as a doctrine of statutory interpretation pertains to the principled objection and the reliability one. Primarily, the objection to intentionalism is a normative one: textualists doubt that legislative intent is a legitimate guide to legal interpretation. The main argument is that intentions or purposes and the like are not what legislators vote on. The law, they claim, is what gets to be voted on by the legislators in the final passage of the bill. Therefore, the content that is democratically enacted is the content expressed by the bill that is voted on, not the various intentions, expectations, and motives that lay behind it.[5]

There is something undeniably true about this argument, but whether it yields the conclusion that textualism seeks to draw from it is questionable. It is undeniably true that, in a democratic legislative assembly, the law enacted is the law voted on; it is the text that gains majority support and passes all of the relevant procedural hurdles. But when a genuine question of statutory interpretation arises, it is usually not a question about what the law says, but about how to complete or modify the statutory law when it is not clear what the law says, or not clear how what it does say settles the dispute at hand. Pointing out that the content of statutory law is the content of the text voted on does not necessarily bear on the question of what judges should do when that content is no longer clear enough to determine a particular legal result. As long as the putative legislative intent is not at odds with what the law says, it does not seem to go against democratic principles to interpret the law according to the intentions of legislators, even if, granted, those intentions were not put to any majority vote.

Nevertheless, there is more than a grain of truth in textualism's qualms about the fairness of intentionalism and its compatibility with democratic principles of legislation. But the argument here cannot be detached from the reliability objection. What seems to be undemocratic about deference to legislative intent is closely tied to the inherent unreliability of it. In most cases, the enactment of a law is a result of bargaining and compromise. Different legislators, representing different constituencies and interests, may want to achieve different things by the law they strive to enact. Typically, the final text voted

[5] See, for example, J. Waldron, *Law and Disagreement*, ch. 6.

on is a result of a compromise, often a rather delicate one at that. The intentions and purposes expressed at various stages of the legislative process are not necessarily reflective of anything that the majority of legislators, or even the majority that supported the bill, would have necessarily assented to. Furthermore, at least in the U.S. Congress, precisely because legislators know that courts tend to defer to legislative intent, they use public expressions of their intentions strategically, attempting to put on the legislative record intentions and purposes that they know are unlikely to get majority support as part of the bill voted on. By relying on the legislative record in order to extract the legislative intent, courts reinforce such manipulative behavior; they allow particular legislators to influence legal results beyond the content that would have gained majority support. Thus, the idea that there is something undemocratic about deference to legislative intent is not entirely without merit. But again, the principled objection cannot be detached from the reliability problem. If there is a context in which the intentions of the legislature as a whole are clear enough, and form part of what the legislature took itself to be enacting, then it is difficult to see any principled, democracy-based objection to courts deferring to the relevant intentions. Textualists, however, would probably be correct to doubt that there are many such cases.[6]

b. Purposivism

The second main doctrine of statutory interpretation that textualists object to is purposivism. This is not really one doctrine but a whole family of views—some made very influential by the Hart and Sacks legal process view, others by Ronald Dworkin—arguing that the task of statutory interpretation should be seen as continuous with the legislative task of making the law in the first place, or, at least, coherent with it.[7] Roughly, the idea is this: when faced with an interpretative question about a statute, judges should ask themselves what the

[6] It is quite possible that the reliability objection is less forceful with respect to parliamentary systems, where most of the legislation is introduced by the government and often passes with little amendment. (See R. Ekins, *The Nature of Legislative Intent.*) These considerations vary with different legal systems and democratic cultures. My arguments in the text pertain mostly to the U.S. congressional system, where legislation is not introduced by the executive branch and, even when it is, in a way, drafting tends to undergo very significant modifications in lieu of bargaining, compromise, and logrolling.

[7] See, for example, H. M. Hart and A. M. Sacks, *The Legal Process* at 1374–81; L. Fuller, *The Morality of Law*; R. M. Dworkin, *Law's Empire.*

relevant purpose of the law is and how that general purpose can best be achieved by resolving the particular interpretative question one way or the other. And how do we know what the relevant purpose of the law is? Not by trying to figure out the actual intentions of the legislators, but by asking what a reasonable legislature would have reasonably wanted to achieve by enacting the piece of legislation that it did. In other words, all forms of purposivism are committed to the stipulation of some idealized conditions under which we conceive of the legislature and the purposes of its enactment. We derive the putative purposes of the law from the facts concerning the circumstances that brought about the legislation, or the mischief it aimed to fix, and, crucially, from some normative assumptions about what a reasonable or morally idealized legislature would have wanted to achieve under those conditions.

Needless to say, views may differ, as they do, about what makes a legislature reasonable and its aims morally legitimate, and about how to determine such matters. I think that the Hart and Sacks view assumed that common sense and reasonably informed, perhaps enlightened and progressive, views about the world would normally suffice. Dworkin is much more elaborate on this issue, and much more explicit in articulating a liberal, moral–political philosophy that, in his view, underlies the constructive model of interpretation he offers. All purposivists emphasize, however, that, in attributing purposes and intentions to a piece of legislation, it is not the actual purposes of the legislators that judges should try to discover, but the purposes or intentions of an idealized, partly normatively constructed legislature.

More or less the same considerations that make purposivism attractive to its proponents make purposivism very suspicious to textualists. Two main kinds of considerations are contentious here. First, textualists object to the very idea that statutory interpretation by the courts ought to be seen as continuous with the process of making the law. The enactment of a law is a democratic process; the judicial interpretation of the law is not. The enactment of a law aims to achieve some policy goals; the judicial interpretation of a statute should have no such aims, as it is not the role of judges to enact new policies. And so on and so forth. Second, textualists seem to be very dubious about the possibility of objectivity concerning the idealized legislative purposes. To quote Scalia again: "Your best shot at figuring out what the legislature meant is to ask yourself what a wise and intelligent person *should* have meant; and that will surely bring you to the conclusion that the law means what you think it *ought* to mean."[8] The emphasis, however, is not on the "ought," where Scalia put it and where Dworkin, for example, would be happy to leave it; it is on the "*you* think," meaning the particular judge who happens to adjudicate the case. In other words, purposivism, according to textualism, is nothing less than an invitation for judges to make the law as they see fit, as *they* think it ought to have been made. And that, according to textualists, is not a legitimate role for the judiciary in a democratic regime.

Needless to say, both of these concerns are serious and both deserve serious answers. I will not attempt to engage with these normative issues here, however, but I will show, in the last section, that textualism faces the same challenges, and that it is not less normatively contentious than purposivism or any other theory of statutory interpretation. But first, we need to see what textualism offers and how it is supposed to work. If neither the actual intentions of legislators nor the putative reasonable purposes of the law are guides to statutory interpretation, what is left for judges to consider? The textualist answer consists in the idea that judges have to rely, first and foremost, on what the relevant statutory provision actually says (and implicates). And what the law says or asserts is determined by what a reasonably informed person, knowing the relevant context and the relevant legal background, would infer from the words expressed by the statute in the context of its expression. In other words, we seek to grasp the meaning of the statutory text in the context of its expression, as that meaning would be grasped by a reasonable hearer aware of the legal and other background conditions of the legislation.[9]

The starting point of textualism is by and large the main thesis presented in chapter 1. Textualism clearly shares the idea that legislation is a speech act, an act of communication, whereby the legislature, by voting on a bill, communicates a certain legal content, and that legal content is the content of the statutory law. And this raises two questions: what are the determinants of communicated content, and how helpful are those determinants in solving the kind of interpretative issues that courts need to decide? In chapters 1 and 2 we tried to answer the first of these questions, and thus the main question to be addressed here is the second one.

[8] A. Scalia, *A Matter of Interpretation*, 18.

[9] See A. Scalia and B. Garner, *Reading Law*, 33; see also J. F. Manning, "What Divides Textualists from Purposivists?" 79–85.

Before we get to the second question, however, let me reiterate one of the controversies we encountered in chapter 1, because it has a special bearing on the coherence of textualism. No doubt, when textualists advise us to look at the meaning of an expression in the context of its utterance, what they have in mind is what we call the *assertive* content of the utterance; it is what the speaker actually says by uttering the expression in the particular context of the speech. But then, according a Gricean view, articulated in this context by Stephen Neale, the content asserted by a speaker just *is* the content that the speaker *intended* to convey to the hearer by expressing the utterance in the particular context that she did.[10] As Neale rightly observes, according to this subjective conception of assertive content, textualism turns out to be incoherent. Once we admit that the context of the expression partly determines what the speaker actually said or asserted—as textualism does—one must concede that context matters precisely because it helps the hearer to figure out the relevant communication intentions of the speaker. Why else would it matter? But then, textualism can no longer deny that what the law actually says is what the legislators intended to say; on the contrary, by trying to ascertain what the law says, we inevitably try to grasp the communication intentions of those who enacted the law.

Textualism, however, seems quite explicit in rejecting this subjective conception of assertive context, and for good reasons. As I argued in chapter 1, any plausible conception of how we characterize assertive content must make room for the possibility that speakers do not necessarily succeed in conveying all that they intend to convey by their utterances; people can simply fail to say exactly what they wanted to say. Therefore, any plausible conception of assertive content must comprise some objective criteria of success. The assertive content of an utterance is determined by what a *reasonable hearer*, knowing the relevant conversational background and context, would infer about the speaker's communication intentions from the words or sentences uttered in that context. It makes perfect sense to define the assertive content of an utterance in a given context by reference to what a reasonable hearer, sharing the relevant contextual background, would infer about the intended content of the utterance in the context of its expression. Furthermore, I think that textualists are quite right to assume that the relevant reasonable hearer, in the

[10] S. Neale, "Textualism with Intent."

context of statutory interpretation, is an adequately informed legal hearer, so to speak—namely, one who is well informed about all the background legal landscape and the technicalities of legal jargon.[11]

Where does this leave the Gricean critique? Neale is correct, I think, up to a point. He is correct to point out that there is a considerable exaggeration in the contrast that textualism aims to emphasize between what the law says and what the lawmakers meant or intended to say. Since textualism admits that, in trying to figure out what the law says, we cannot be content with the semantic content of the relevant expression, and that we must be guided by various pragmatic factors in trying to determine the assertive content of the relevant legal provision, textualism has already conceded that the communication intentions of the lawmakers are what we aim to ascertain. A hearer who wants to grasp what the speaker says aims to grasp what the speaker intended to communicate; legal speech cannot be a kind of striking exception. However, I do not think that textualism needs to deny this point. All it needs to say in response is that the main issue here is whether we rely on a purely subjective conception of assertive content or on an objective conception. As long as textualism endorses the objective view, which it clearly does, it is entitled to the conclusion that what the law says is not fully determined by what its enactors intended to say. In other words, textualism can concede the idea that legal interpretation aims to ascertain the communication intentions of the legislature, as long as it is granted that the relevant communication intentions are understood objectively—that is, as they would be grasped by a reasonable hearer.

2. How Helpful Is Textualism?

So far so good. Textualism tells us that statutory law consists in what the law says, what it actually asserts. And, at least in my mind, textualism seems to rely on a very plausible conception of what assertive content is—namely, an objective one. But now the main question is, how helpful is all this as a theory of statutory interpretation? It is not all that helpful, I will argue, because it is not frequently the case that a question of statutory interpretation arises due to some plausible question about the assertive content of the relevant legal expression.

[11] See Scalia and Garner, and Manning, note 9 above.

In most cases of statutory interpretation, the problem is not that we are not quite sure about what the law says; the problems arise because what the law says is not sufficient to determine how to resolve the particular dilemma that the court faces.

Now the obvious step here is to look into the kind of cases that give rise to some indeterminacy of statutory law, and see whether the tools offered by textualism have any bearing on how such cases can be resolved. In other words, we need to see what kind of problems engender the need for interpretation of statutory law. The main problems are vagueness, of course, conflict of laws, ambiguity (and polysemy), and implicated content. As I will try to show, textualism has no tools in its shed to deal with any of these forms of interpretative challenges. We have already discussed vagueness in detail in the previous chapter, and saw that a great deal of indeterminacy in statutory law stems from various forms of vagueness, some deliberately chosen by legislatures and some inadvertent or inevitable. I hope it is clear from our discussion in chapter 4 that, when courts face a borderline case of a vague term in a statute, language is not going to be helpful in the precisification required by the court. Trying to pay closer attention to what the law says, in such cases, is like hoping to get richer by gazing at your wallet. So let me consider in some detail the other types of cases.

a. Conflicting regulations

Laws may come into conflict in several ways. The simplest form of conflict concerns cases in which different laws require an agent to perform different and mutually exclusive things under a given set of circumstances. For example, consider these two laws:

L1: "All Xs who are F ought to φ in circumstances C."

L2: "All Xs who are G ought to ψ in circumstances C."

And now assume two additional facts. First, that it is practically impossible to do both φ and ψ in the same set of circumstances. Second, assume that there is an X, say *Xa*, who happens to be both an F and a G. According to L1, *Xa* is required to φ, whereas, according to L2, *Xa* is required to ψ. Assuming that one cannot both φ and ψ in C, the two laws conflict: they require an agent to do and not to do something under the same set of circumstances. Sometimes there is a third law determining which one of these conflicting regulations prevails in such cases of conflict. But not always, and when there is no such additional regulation about how to resolve the conflict, a genuine conflict remains, usually for the courts to figure out. Needless to say, there is very little about the meaning of the expressions in their context that can help the courts to resolve such genuine practical conflicts between different laws. What the two laws say might be as clear as possible; the problem is that the relevant agent just cannot comply with both of them. And then, presumably, the courts would need to determine which one of the conflicting laws is more important to comply with under the pertinent circumstances.

Laws may come into conflict, however, in more subtle ways than this. An example we discussed in chapter 2, concerning the litigation of the TVA dam, demonstrates that laws may come into conflict in their respective presuppositions. By allocating funds to the construction of the dam in its appropriation bills, Congress clearly conveyed the presupposition that it deemed the project legally authorized. However, by enacting the Endangered Species Act, Congress conveyed the message that the authority to make decisions about construction projects with certain environmental impacts is in the hands of the Environmental Protection Agency (EPA)—or Fish and Wildlife Service (FWS), as the case may be—and no longer held by Congress. As we saw in chapter 2, these two messages came into conflict in the TVA case. Similarly, the example we discussed at the end of chapter 4, *FDA v. Brown & Williamson*, also shows how different presuppositions of congressional acts may come into conflict: on the one hand, Congress gave the Food and Drug Administration (FDA) very broad authority to regulate any substance that is intended to "affect the ... function of the body"; on the other hand, Congress enacted several bills regulating the advertisement and sale of cigarettes and other tobacco products, clearly thereby presupposing that it is legal to produce and sell them. However, as we noted in discussing the case, the relevant part of the statute regulating the FDA made it mandatory for the FDA to ban the sale of tobacco if it falls within its jurisdiction. Thus, on the one hand, we have a series of laws clearly presupposing that the sale of tobacco products is legal; on the other hand, we have a jurisdictional regulation that would entail a mandatory requirement to ban their sale. Once again, it is difficult to see how textualism would have any tools at its disposal to deal with such cases. None of them depends on how we grasp what the law says, or even how we interpret what the law implicates, precisely because the implications involved here are in conflict with each other.[12]

b. Ambiguity and polysemy

Of all the various types of linguistic indeterminacy we find in statutory law, ambiguity would seem to be the kind of case that lends itself to the textualist method. Ambiguity concerns those cases in which an expression has two possible, though unrelated, meanings. Normally, when we face an ambiguous expression, the assumption is that the speaker *intended* to use one of the two possible meanings; disambiguation, whether by context or other pragmatic factors, aims at figuring out the communication intention of the speaker in the specific context of the utterance. There are two main types of ambiguity in a natural language: syntactical and lexical.[13] As an example of syntactical ambiguity, consider the sentence: "I know a man who has a dog who has fleas." The sentence can be read in two ways: either the man has fleas or the dog has them, and, by itself, the sentence is indeterminate between these options. Lexical ambiguity concerns those cases in which a given word has two separate and unrelated meanings in the natural language in question, such as the word "bank" in English, meaning, in one sense, the side of a river and, in a very different sense, a financial institution. As I mentioned in chapter 1, the contextual knowledge required to disambiguate lexical ambiguity is often general and widely shared; it does not have to be specific to the particular conversation in question. A directive regulating the opening hours of

[12] It is interesting to note that Scalia was resonantly silent in the FDA case. He joined the majority opinion in favor of the tobacco industry, without saying a word on how the decision squares with the language of the law.

[13] Actually, there is a third, pragmatic type of ambiguity, particularly with respect to the use of definite descriptions (and some cases of proper names). As Kripke ("Speaker's Reference and Semantic Reference") and others have argued, Donnellan's famous ambiguity between referential and attributive uses of definite descriptions ("Reference and Definite Descriptions") is most likely a pragmatic ambiguity concerning a speaker's meaning/intention, not semantics. Potentially, such a pragmatic ambiguity in the use of definite descriptions might be present in law as well. But very rarely, actually. When a statute employs a definite description (such as "the governor of California"), it is quite obviously an attributive use, squarely within the Russellian account. Referential uses of definite descriptions in statutory law would be very rare. My guess is that we will only find them in the context of an incomplete definite description (such as "the table," or "the tax," etc.) embedded within a syntactically complex expression, and then it would be in essence a singular proposition, referring to some object picked out by other parts of the sentence. (E.g., "income tax on earnings of $X is Y% and the tax has to be added to...," where, clearly, the incomplete definite description, "the tax," simply refers to the income tax mentioned earlier in the expression.)

"banks" would refer to financial institutions, not river banks, and we know this simply because we know that river banks have no opening hours, while commercial institutions do. In other cases, disambiguation may require contextual knowledge that is specific to the particular conversation in question.

It is possible, however, to extend the idea of semantic ambiguity to include expressions that have become idiomatically or colloquially ambiguous, even if they are not lexically so. Suppose, for example, that somebody asks me whether I use drugs. That depends, I would reply. If by "drugs" you mean hallucinatory substances, the answer is no. But if by "drugs" you mean to include medications, then, yes, I regularly use prescription drugs. The word "drug" is not lexically ambiguous (like "bank"), because the two meanings are closely related, but it has come to be used, idiomatically in English, in a way that is, in effect, ambiguous. And this phenomenon is, I think, quite common, though how far it extends is not entirely clear.

Be this as it may, it is not difficult to see that textualism would have something to say about the way to handle ambiguity in statutory law. When faced with an ambiguous expression, we should ask ourselves which one of the two possible meanings of the expression in question is the one actually *communicated* in the specific context of the expression. And, normally, the right answer is not very difficult to surmise. Standard lexical ambiguity is rarely a problem in law. Since the standard case of lexical ambiguity concerns words whose different meanings are unrelated, the context of the law is usually clear enough to determine which one of the two meanings of the word was intended by the legislature. Syntactical ambiguity is a bit more prevalent, and typically inadvertent. Legislatures make an effort to avoid syntactical ambiguities; sometimes they fail, of course, which is typically unfortunate, as syntactical ambiguity serves no useful purpose.[14]

A much more prevalent aspect of meaning, however, is *polysemy*. Consider, for example, the following two sets of utterances:

(1a) "I broke the window" (the window's glass).

(1b) "I opened the window" (the window's inner frame with the glass).

[14] At least in the U.S., judges and lawyers seem to be utterly confused about the distinction between ambiguity and vagueness; every linguistic indeterminacy they tend to call ambiguity. They see an ambiguity wherever a case can be made to understand a statutory expression in more than one way.

(1c) "I entered through the window" (the window's outer frame).

(2a) "John struggled to pull the cart out of the mud" (physical effort).

(2b) "John struggled to finish his dissertation in time" (intellectual effort).

As these examples demonstrate, the objects or features that words pick out within their definite extension—"window" in (1) and "struggle" in (2)—can vary with circumstances and contexts of expression. According to some views in semantics, polysemy is not an exception but the rule; the meaning of words, the information they encode, is very minimal, and hearers almost always work out the relevant meaning in the context of the conversation as they go along. As I mentioned in chapter 1, I do not think that this minimalist (or sometimes called contextualist) semantics view is quite right, but it is not my purpose to argue either way. Suffice it for our purposes to say that words often designate a particular subset of their semantic range, depending on the speaker's intentions and the particular context of the conversation in which they are used. In some cases, polysemy is the opposite of vagueness; we face a sorties sequence when we need to extend the application of a word beyond its core, definite extension. Polysemy, on the other hand, often arises when the speaker refers only to a particular subset of the definite extension. (But this is not always true: sometimes the distinction between polysemy and figurative or metaphoric use of a word is not all that clear.[15])

Consider the famous case of *Smith v. United States*.[16] The relevant statute mandated a much harsher punishment for drug-related crimes if the defendant was "using a firearm" during the drug-related activity. In the *Smith* case, the defendant used a firearm in a barter deal in exchange for the drugs. So the question was whether using a firearm

[15] Consider, for example, the various uses of the word "man," such as in, "John finally behaved like a man" (man as stereotype); "Marriage is a contract between a man and a woman" (man as adult male or gender); "Socrates is a man and therefore mortal" (man as a member of *Homo sapiens*). These kinds of examples are often given as examples of polysemy, and surely there is a sense in which they are. But the use of "man" to stand for a stereotype can also be analyzed as a quasi-figurative use, one that goes beyond the definite extension of the meaning of the word. Thus, I am inclined to think that there are two types of polysemy: a narrow type, which concerns intended extensions within the definite extension of the word, and a wide one, which includes quasi-figurative uses of words and various other forms of stretching the word's extension beyond its standard meaning.

[16] 508 U.S. 223 (1993). Scalia's dissent in *Smith* is one of the textbook examples of textualism in statutory interpretation, almost always invoked in this context.

as an object of value, not as a weapon, counts as "using a firearm" in connection with a drug deal. The majority decided affirmatively, but in a famous dissent, Scalia argued that there is no linguistic indeterminacy here whatsoever. Using an object is normally understood as using it for its intended purpose or function, not for just any use whatsoever. Hence he argued that the expression "using a firearm" only applies to cases in which the firearm is used as a weapon, not as an object of value for a barter deal. His main argument was based on the thesis that "using a firearm" is simply not ambiguous. And, in a sense, though a different sense from what he meant, Scalia is right; this case is about polysemy, not ambiguity.

Consider again the pair of sentences:

(a) "John struggled to pull his cart out of the mud."
(b) "John struggled to finish his dissertation on time."

Two points are worth noting here. The word "struggle" in (a) stands for something different from "struggle" in (b). However, the word "struggle" is polysemous, not ambiguous; the two meanings in context are closely related, well within the semantic range of the word. In this respect, I think that Scalia is quite right about the fact that there is no ambiguity involved in "using a firearm." In fact, we can easily construct a similar pair of sentences about the expression "using an x":

(a★) "Jane uses a laptop."
(b★) "Jane uses a laptop to keep the door open."

We can assume that (a★) refers to using the laptop as a computer, and with equal certainty we can infer that in (b★) the laptop is used as a doorstop. In short, it is quite right that the expression "using an x" is not semantically ambiguous. The problem in *Smith* is about polysemy. The word "use" has a very wide semantic range; when we use an expression like "using an x," we may designate a specific subset of the word's definite extension. And in most cases, this is clear enough from the meaning of the relevant sentence, combined with our background knowledge of relevant aspects of the world.

Having said this, Scalia's conclusion might be correct if it is generally the case that a non-anaphoric use of "use" is normally understood in a restricted extension within the wide semantic range of the word. If it is generally true that an expression of the form "A uses an x" is understood by default in the restricted sense of using the x for x's typical purpose or function, then Scalia is right. And that seems quite plausible. Technically speaking, this is probably an example of what Grice called "generalized conversational implicature," discussed in chapter 2. The expression "A uses an x," without anaphora, would normally implicate that A uses the x for x's typical function or purpose.

However, I doubt that this is generally the case with similar examples of polysemy. Notice that this does not work with words like "struggle." The expression "A struggled to φ" does not indicate what kind of effort "struggle" designates if we do not know the nature of φ. Or consider the case often mentioned in parallel with *Smith*, *Muscarello v. U.S.*:[17] the question was whether "carrying a firearm" in relation to a drug deal applies to carrying it in the trunk of the defendant's car. Once again, Scalia used the same argument to conclude that it does not. But here I think that he was mistaken. I doubt that the expression "carrying an x," without anaphoric addition, by default refers to carrying it on one's body. If I ask a driver who happens to have a flat tire, "Are you carrying a spare tire?" he would respond quite sensibly by saying, "Yes, it's in the trunk of my car." Or the sentence, "The accident victim was carried to the hospital," would certainly not imply that he was carried on somebody's person. When I ask my wife whether she happens to carry some cash with her, I would refer to carrying it in her purse, of course, not in the trunk of her car. But that is so because we know that people normally carry cash in their wallet or purse. In other words, polysemy applies to words used in a given context to designate a particular subset of objects within the word's semantic range. The relevant context is typically given by our general background knowledge of how things are in the world. The context does not have to be specific to the particular conversation in question. However, it is not generally the case, as Scalia seems to assume, that by default non-anaphoric expressions of such words are normally understood in a restricted, narrow sense. It all depends on the nature of the object or instance on which the word is predicated, and things we generally know about the relevant aspects of the world. To conclude: from a semantic perspective, Scalia's reasoning was probably correct in *Smith*, but incorrect in *Muscarello*. And I suspect that most cases of polysemy are like the latter.

[17] 524 U.S. 125 (1998).

Either way, in determining which one of the subset extensions is relevant to the expression uttered, we aim to grasp the communication intention of the speaker. Speakers (talking literally, that is, without irony or metaphor) are normally free to use a polysemous word to designate any particular subset within the semantic range of the word they use, and communication succeeds when the hearer can grasp the intended extension. Therefore, when Congress enacts a law using words with different possible extensions, and the court is tasked with figuring out the relevant extension of the word in the context of the specific law in question, it is difficult to see how such a determination could avoid an attempt to figure out the lawmaker's intentions. I am not suggesting that courts would need to rely on external evidence about legislative intent; on the contrary, as I suggested above, the pragmatic determinants are often on the surface, evident from general contextual knowledge widely shared. But the result of such inferences is inevitably about communication intentions. The contrast that textualism flags between what the law means and what the legislators have meant is spurious in most of these cases. What the law means, in the sense of its intended extension, is what the lawmakers intended; if they have had no such intentions, as is quite possible in the cases of *Smith* and *Muscarello*, then there is simply no answer to the question of what the law means. It can mean either one of the options, and a choice has to be made on the basis of the relevant normative considerations. Paying closer attention to semantic meaning in cases of polysemy is, again, like gazing at your wallet hoping to find more money in it. Looking more carefully at what such words "ordinarily mean" is not helpful.

c. *Legal implicatures*

Textualists have long noted that, in addition to what the law says or asserts, it may also implicate some content that goes beyond what it actually says. Emphasizing the potential role of implicated content in the legislative context has become one of the trademarks of textualism, a central tool it proposes in solving cases of statutory interpretation. The attraction of this move is easy to discern. On the one hand, it allows textualism to go beyond what the law explicitly says, showing that, even if it does not actually say something relevant to the case at hand, it might have implicated it. On the other hand, such implications are relevant, textualism can claim, because they are part of what the law actually communicates; after all, implicatures and utterance presuppositions are contents communicated by an expression in the context of its utterance. So the idea is that we can remain within the bounds of communicated content yet often find that the law conveys more than it actually asserts. Implicatures and utterance presuppositions, on this view, form part and parcel of what "the law promulgates"—namely, of its communicated content.

In their book, *Reading Law*, Scalia and Garner list fifty-seven canons of construction that they claim apply in U.S. law. Some of these canons, as linguists have noted, are ordinary Gricean conversational maxims or close relatives of them.[18] Consider, for example, the oft-quoted canon of construction *expressio unius est exlusio alterius* (the expression of one thing implies the exclusion of others). As Scalia demonstrates, "when a car dealer promises a low financing to 'purchasers with good credit,' it is entirely clear that the rate is not available to purchasers with spotty credit."[19] Fancy Latin phraseology notwithstanding, this is quite simply the Gricean maxim of quantity: do not say too little. Thus the idea is that the law already incorporates, by way of established canons of construction, the Gricean mechanism of conversational implicatures, enabling the courts to infer implicated content of legislation beyond its asserted content.

To be sure, the canons of construction that Scalia lists in his book are not only maxims of conversation—in fact, very few of them are. Some are special and widely recognized rules of legislative drafting, such as the rule that phrases in masculine formulation include the feminine. Most other canons they list, however, are substantive legal doctrines (e.g., "presumption against waiver of sovereign immunity," or the *mens rea* canon, etc.). I will have nothing to say about the long list of substantive legal doctrines that Scalia calls canons of construction, nor would I press the obvious question: why not subsume countless other legal doctrines under canon formulations and give us a list of hundreds of them? The essential point, for our purposes, is that textualism seems to maintain that the legal content of statutes includes not only the kind of content that is actually asserted by the law, but also content that is implicated by it. Furthermore, textualism's explicit assumption here is that, by relying on canons of construction and ordinary inferences to implicated content, judges can avoid the normative and potentially controversial forms of reasoning

18 See, for example, R. A. Carston, "Legal Texts and Canons of Construction."

19 A. Scalia and B. Garner, *Reading Law*, 107.

that plague purposivism and intentionalism. But both of these ideas are questionable.

The main problem for textualism here should be evident from the lessons we learned in chapter 2. We have seen that legislative discourse is strategic in nature and therefore it cannot be simply assumed that the ordinary Gricean maxims of cooperative conversations apply to legislative speech. As I argued in chapter 2, the inference to implicated content in the law is much less secure than inference to implicated content in the ordinary types of conversation where parties aim at a truthful exchange of information.

Why could textualism not maintain, however, that the nature of the conversation between the courts and the legislature is a fully cooperative one or, at least, should be assumed to be so? The answer is that it is an essential part of textualism's rationale, its raison d'état, to assume the strategic nature of the conversation here; after all, textualism repeatedly emphasizes the distinction between what the legislators may have wanted to convey and what they have actually succeeded in conveying, giving legal effect only to the latter. Had we assumed a fully cooperative type of conversation between the legislatures and the courts, intentionalism (and to some extent purposivism) would have won the day, and it would make much more sense to strive to ascertain what it is that the legislature wished to accomplish, rather than focusing on what it said. After all, in an ordinary conversation, where parties are fully cooperative, it is precisely each other's intentions that parties to the conversation try to figure out, not only, or even mainly, what is said or asserted. Furthermore, the strategic nature of the conversation between legislators themselves during the enactment process forms an essential part of the reliability argument against intentionalism that textualism relies on. Pointing out the inherent difficulties of trying to ascertain what legislators may have wanted to convey and the inevitable unreliability of such attempts heavily draws on the strategic nature of the legislative process. In other words, an essential part of the appeal of textualism crucially depends on the strategic nature of legislative discourse and the idea that the conversation between courts and legislature cannot be modeled on an ordinary conversation between friends, as it were.

The problem, of course, is that if we assume that the conversation is strategic, rather than fully cooperative, then the norms that govern the conversation become somewhat questionable, and, in any case, the determination of what would count as content that has been implicated by a given utterance becomes very uncertain. Now, this would seem to entail that textualism should be much more skeptical about content that is allegedly implicated, but not quite asserted, by a piece of legislative utterance; but such skepticism comes with a high price, as it would deplete textualism even further of its otherwise meager resources in dealing with the variety of statutory interpretation challenges that judges face. We have already noted that textualism has no resources to deal with interpretative questions stemming from vagueness and polysemy; it has no resources to deal with conflict between different laws, especially when the asserted content of each is in no serious doubt. And, though this is an issue I have not dealt with here, textualism's record on dealing with cases where what the law actually says yields absurd results is uneven at best.[20] In short, textualism turns out to be a very minimal interpretative tool, one that is simply not going to help judges solve most of the actual problems they face in statutory interpretation.

One may suspect that we have come a long way only to point out something that should have been obvious from the start: textualism tells judges to focus on what the law actually says or asserts, rather than on speculations about what legislatures may have wanted to say, or what the reasonable purpose of the law may have been. Litigants, however, are not going to waste their time and money on litigation only to be told something they could easily have figured out by themselves. If cases dealing with statutory interpretation reach the courts (especially appellate courts), it is either because it is not sufficiently clear, under the circumstances, what the law says, or else because what the law says is clear enough but is not sufficient to determine the result of the interpretative question that arises. Not many cases, to put it cautiously, really depend on grasping what the relevant statutory phrase simply says or asserts in the context of its utterance.[21]

[20] There is a striking dissonance between the stance Scalia takes in his writings about this issue and his actual judicial decisions. In his writings, Scalia clearly indicates that it is not the job of judges to correct the mistakes of the legislature when unintended and unforeseen consequences of their legislative language result in absurd consequences. But in some of his own rulings, Scalia has done just that—namely, corrected legislative formulation to avoid absurdity. See, for example, *Green v. Bock Laundry Co.* (1989) and *FDA v. Brown & Williamson* (2000). Judge Easterbrook is much more consistent with his view that absurd results do not count against clear legislative language. See his majority opinion in *Marshall v. U.S.* (1990) Court of Appeals 7th Circuit.

[21] Almost every discussion about textualism ends up with only a handful of examples of actual Supreme Court cases from the last few decades, invariably discussing *Smith v. U.S.* and three or four others. There is no abundance of examples where textualism is actually in play.

So it seems that textualism, though plausible within the narrow confines of articulating the determinants of what the law says, is rather unhelpful and vacuous as a general theory of statutory interpretation. But this is no accident; the debate between various theories of statutory interpretation is as much about political morality as it is about language and interpretation. And the debate is mostly about the level of cooperation that should be practiced between the legislature and the courts. Purposivism and intentionalism purport to be guided by a strong cooperative principle, whereby the role of the courts in interpreting the law is seen as continuous with the legislative process, aiming to give effect to the policy goals that the legislature strove to achieve. Textualism rejects, on moral–political grounds, this strong cooperative principle; it wants the courts to deal with the legislature at arm's length. The role of judges, on this view, is not to complete the project that the legislature has started, so to speak, but to implement what the legislature ordered, regardless of the policy goals that may have guided it. In other words, textualism is unhelpful as a theory of statutory interpretation at least in part because it does not want to be helpful, or at least not more than absolutely necessary. I am not trying to argue here that this is necessarily a wrong moral–political stance (or a right one), only to emphasize that it is just as political and just as normatively contentious as any of its rivals. Different moral–political understandings of democracy, and the values inherent in democratic legislation, yield different views about the appropriate role of the judiciary in a democratic regime. Textualism can present itself as avoiding the contentious normative considerations that seem inevitable in purposive statutory interpretation only because it relies on a certain vision of democracy that is, however, not less politically contentious than any other. Morality and politics form an integral part of statutory interpretation on any plausible view of it; the differences are in the morality, and the politics, to which judges subscribe.

6

Meaning and Belief in Constitutional Interpretation

The distinction between a *concept* and its different *conceptions* plays a prominent role in debates about constitutional interpretation. Proponents of a dynamic reading of the Constitution—espousing interpretation of constitutional concepts according to their contemporary understandings—typically rely on the idea that the Constitution entrenches only the general *concepts* it deploys, without authoritatively favoring any particular *conception* of it, and, in particular, without favoring the particular conception of the relevant concept that the framers of the Constitution may have had in mind. Originalists argue, to the contrary, that fidelity to the Constitution requires an understanding of its provisions according to the particular conception of the abstract concepts prevalent at the time of enactment, and not those we may now favor.

The concept versus conceptions distinction is closely related to other kinds of vagueness and polysemy that we find in statutory language. My main purpose in this chapter is to put some pressure on the linguistic considerations that are presented in this constitutional context, arguing that they are much more problematic than the proponents of both positions assume. I will try to show that the debate here is actually a moral–political one, mostly about the main rationale of a constitutional regime and the conditions of its legitimacy. It is, primarily, a debate about what constitutions are for, and what makes them legitimate. But I will only get to this moral issue at the end. The main part of the chapter will strive to show that the semantic considerations employed in this debate are inconclusive; the way concepts are used in a given context depends on various pragmatic determinants, and those, in turn, depend on the nature of the conversation in question. The moral disagreement is, ultimately, about the kind of conversation that constitutional regimes are taken to establish.

1. The Scalia–Dworkin Debate

The debate about constitutional interpretation between Scalia and Dworkin provides a good starting point for our discussion. Scalia is a textualist about statutory interpretation and an originalist (of sorts) about constitutional interpretation. Many are puzzled by this combination, which seems contradictory on its face. Textualism, as we saw in chapter 5, urges judges to focus on what the statutory provision *says*, as opposed to what the legislators may have *meant* to say; what the legislators may have intended to say, supposedly learned by consulting the legislative history of the statute under consideration, is regarded by textualism as legally irrelevant, something that should not be brought to bear on the appropriate interpretation of statutory law. But when it comes to constitutional interpretation, we seem to get the opposite view: originalism is the view that constitutional provisions are to be understood as they would have been understood by the framers of the Constitution and their contemporary audience. Indeed, when you look at Scalia's decisions and opinions on constitutional matters, you often see an essay in legal history, exegetically examining historical clues in order to extract some views about the ways in which constitutional provisions were understood at the time of their enactment. So if legislative history should be irrelevant to statutory interpretation, why is it relevant, indeed central, to constitutional interpretation?

The truth of the matter is that there is less inconsistency here than meets the eye. According to textualism, the main operative factor in statutory interpretation is what the law actually says or asserts. As I explained in chapter 5, textualism explicitly endorses an objective conception of the assertive content of an utterance. What the law says is at least partly determined by what a reasonable hearer, knowing all the relevant background, would infer that it says. In other words, textualism can concede the idea that legal interpretation aims to ascertain the communication intentions of the legislature, as long as it is granted that the relevant communication intentions are understood objectively. Now, if you add to this the relevant timeframe, which is presumed to be the time of enactment, you can begin to see how legislative history might become relevant to constitutional interpretation or, in fact, to any piece of legislation that is relatively old. The purpose of the historical exegesis is to ascertain what a reasonable hearer at the time of enactment would have inferred that the constitutional provision says. Thus, Scalia could claim, with some plausibility, that in both statutory and constitutional interpretation, the task is the same: try to ascertain what the law says, what it actually asserts. In both cases, assertive content is understood objectively, as it would be grasped by a reasonable hearer knowing all the relevant background in the context of the utterance. The only difference is that, with old enactments, the relevant context and legislative background are less clear; language itself may have changed over time and therefore some historical context is needed in order to figure out what the old law or constitutional provision would have meant to a reasonable hearer at the time of its enactment.[1]

Dworkin is doubtful, however, that the position here is really consistent, because it trades on an ambiguity between two possible forms of textualism.[2] John Perry has recently proposed a very similar argument, and in what follows I will use his terminology. Perry calls these two views "meaning-textualism" and "conception-textualism," respectively.[3] The difference between these views concerns the question of whether or not the assertive content of a legal prescription employing a general evaluative concept also includes the particular conceptions that the enactors associated with the concept.

Perry gives the example of a departmental decision to make "philosophical talent" the main consideration in the department's hiring policy for the future. Now, let us assume that most, or perhaps even all, the members who voted for this resolution took it for granted that philosophical talent consists in analytical rigor, logical skills, a high level of technical sophistication, etc. According to meaning-textualism,

[1] To be sure, I am not claiming that in his judicial opinions Scalia actually follows this rationale. Many of his opinions refer to historical evidence that can only be taken as evidence about the framers' further intentions, motives, or purposes, and the like.

[2] In A. Scalia, *A Matter of Interpretation* at 119. A similar point is found in Dworkin's *Freedom's Law*, ch. 1.

[3] J. Perry, "Textualism and the Discovery of Rights."

the view that Perry favors, none of these specific conceptions of what philosophical talent consists in forms part of the resolution. Thus, for example, if over the years the department's character changes, and it becomes more skeptical of logic and analytical rigor, future members would be warranted in implementing their own bona fide views about what philosophical talent is and would rightly consider their new policy as faithfully implementing the resolution to be guided by "philosophical talent." Conception-textualism, on the other hand, would have us maintain that the resolution to be guided by "philosophical talent" also includes the enactors' particular conception of what philosophical talent consists in. And this view, according to Perry, makes no sense.[4]

The distinction Perry draws here is exactly the same as the one exemplified by Dworkin with the constitutional question about the Fourteenth Amendment and school segregation. We know with considerable certainty that the framers (very broadly construed, if you will) of the Fourteenth Amendment's equal protection clause did not think for a moment that racial segregation in schools violates it; we know that their conception of equal protection would have allowed for the doctrine of "separate but equal" to stand as constitutionally valid. Therefore, if we followed the idea of conception-textualism, we would have to conclude that *Brown v. Board of Education* was wrongly decided. And, I take it, nobody would want to say that.[5] Dworkin and Perry share the view that a consistent and plausible textualism would have us read the constitutional provisions in their abstract formulation as enacting only the general concept, not the particular conception of it that may have been shared by the enactors, or indeed, by the population at large, at that time. To take another example, the asserted content of the Eighth Amendment—what this amendment *says* by prohibiting "cruel and unusual" punishment—is, according to Dworkin, to render any punishment that *is* in fact cruel unconstitutional, and not "punishments widely regarded as cruel and unusual at the date of this enactment."[6]

All of this sounds very sensible. But it would be a mistake to conclude that Dworkin and Perry win the argument by commonsense

[4] J. Perry, "Textualism and the Discovery of Rights" at 109.

[5] In some lectures and conversations, Scalia has admitted, I am told, that the case of *Brown v. Board of Education* poses a serious challenge for his views on constitutional interpretation.

[6] R. M. Dworkin, in Scalia, *A Matter of Interpretation* at 120.

linguistic considerations, as they seem to suggest. Undoubtedly, they are correct to point out that textualism (in statutory interpretation) and originalism (in constitutional interpretation) make for strange bedfellows. But "meaning-textualism" is not more workable or linguistically compelling than "conception-textualism."

The distinction between a concept and its conceptions seems fairly compelling at the phenomenological level. Surely it seems right to say that people can have very different and even mutually exclusive conceptions of general evaluative terms. People can talk about the same thing, such as, say, "justice," while profoundly disagreeing about what justice is, what it requires, etc.[7] Furthermore, we often have a clear sense that such disagreements are reasonable. There is a certain *conceptual tolerance*, as I will call it, that we associate with the concept versus conceptions distinction, whereby we assume that rational people can have reasonable disagreements about their favored conception of a given evaluative concept. You can think that justice is all about what people deserve, in some sense, while I can think that desert is a confused idea and justice has nothing to do with it. And yet we have a sense that we are not necessarily talking past each other, that, in spite of the fact that we have different and incompatible conceptions of justice, we are disagreeing about the appropriate conception of one and the same concept.

Notice, however, that the concept versus conceptions distinction, in this form, does not apply to just about any general concept we have. It would be strange to say that we can have different and incompatible conceptions of "chairs," or that we can have mutually incompatible conceptions of "red" or "redness." But even in the case of general evaluative concept-words, where the concept versus conceptions distinction seems to be most at home, the distinction raises questions: how can we have conflicting views about what, say, justice is, while still talking about the same thing? What is *the thing* we are talking about if we understand it very differently? In short, what does it mean "to share a concept of X" when we profoundly disagree about X's extension, about what "X" designates or stands for?

I will suggest that there are two main answers, one of which is an *externalist* approach, modeled on Putnam's theory of natural kind predicates, and another, which we can call *internalism* about conceptions,

[7] As far as I can tell, the distinction between concept and conceptions (of justice, actually) was first used, though perhaps not quite introduced by, John Rawls in his *A Theory of Justice*.

modeled on Gallie's ideas about essentially contested concepts. The next two sections are devoted to explaining these models and some of the problems they give rise to in the present context.

2. The Externalist Model: Natural Kinds

To share a concept, I will assume here, is tantamount to knowing what the word means in the natural language in question. It is the ability to use the word correctly, if you like. Some philosophers tend to assume that the concept of X is somewhat different from the meaning of the word designating X. Perhaps it is the mental representation or some kind of a mental image of what X, or the thought about it, is. I doubt that this is a helpful way of talking about concepts, but I will not press the issue here.[8] I will assume, however, that people share a concept when they know what the relevant word means in their natural language. To have a concept of X is, or at least requires, if you prefer, to know what "X" means. Meaning, however, is a public feature of language use; words have meanings in virtue of our ability to use them more or less the same way across speakers/hearers and different sentences in which the word appears.

Therefore, we can only use words in a natural language if we share some beliefs about what the word stands for, its extension, with other speakers. Knowing the meaning of a word or how to use it correctly requires speakers to know what, by and large, other speakers believe about the extension of the word. In fact, generally speaking, collectively held beliefs about what a word stands for, what it signifies, are *constitutive* of the word's meaning. Needless to say, individual speakers can use many words in ordinary conversations without knowing all there is to know about the extension of the word, and often they do not need to know the nature of the extension in great detail or very accurately. In most cases, however, including in our use of general categories or kinds, the meaning of the word is presumed to fix the extension (or atleast the definite extension) of the word, the kind of things or objects the word clearly applies to, if used correctly. Therefore, if you know what a word means you know what it stands for, what its extension is. That is generally the case. However, there is a particular

[8] See my "Farewell to Conceptual Analysis (in Jurisprudence)."

kind of words, identified by Hilary Putnam and Saul Kripke, in the 1970s, where the relation between meaning and extension goes the other way around—namely, in the case of *natural kinds*.[9]

Putnam's theory of natural kind words has convincingly shown us that there are many words in our language that we intend to use, as a matter of collective linguistic intention—that is, in a way that purports to designate some kind of things, whatever their real nature turns out to be. With natural kinds, such as "tiger," "water," or "gold," over time we observe some regularities that we assume are somehow connected; we assume that some hidden properties in the nature of things make them what they are, or make them the kind of things they are. And then this kind or category is designated by a word, whereby we take that word to "rigidly" designate whatever the nature of the kind really is, in a way that is essentially externalist. In other words, the designation of the extension of the word is such that it assumes externalism—namely, it assumes that whether an object is of the relevant kind/predicate or not depends on the constitutive role played by whatever it really is that makes things of that kind, irrespective of widely shared beliefs about the nature of the extension. And this entails that we can know what a natural kind word means, collectively as language users, that is, while entertaining inaccurate and perhaps even fundamentally mistaken theories about its extension. The extension of the word is taken to be determined by the true nature of its constitutive elements, whatever they really are.[10] (Since it is probably not the case that any rigid designation (à la Kripke) involves externalism, I will henceforth designate the kind of externalist rigid designation of extension that is involved in natural kinds as "rigid★."[11])

Admittedly, Putnam has also come to the view that people who use natural kind words in their idiolect must share certain beliefs about the nature of the extension of the word, which he called

[9] Two clarifications. First, natural kinds are not the only exception to meaning fixing the reference; for example, proper names (which were the main focus of Kripke's analysis) and pure indexicals also pose exceptions, though in different ways. Second, we should bear in mind that such fixing of reference might be temporal and it can change over time. However, if the use of a given word changes over time to designate different things, then we would say that the meaning of the word changed over time; it now means something else (e.g., "meat," in English, used to mean food, in general; now it means only a subset of food made of the flesh of animals).

[10] The main presentation of this theory is in H. Putnam, *Mind, Language and Reality*, mostly "The Meaning of 'Meaning'," ch. 12.

[11] See S. Soames, *Philosophical Essays, Vol. 2*, ch. 7.

stereotypes: "someone who knows what 'tiger' means ... is *required* to know that *stereotypical* tigers are striped. More precisely, there is one stereotype of tigers (he may have others) that is required by the linguistic community as such; he is required to have this stereotype, and to know (implicitly) that it is obligatory. The stereotype must include the feature of stripes if his acquisition is to count as successful."[12]

I doubt that Putnam is entirely right about this. It is probably true that, in most cases, speakers of a natural language are required to know some salient features of a stereotypical token of a type in order to be able to use the type-word in their everyday lives.[13] (And perhaps this is all that Putnam meant to say here.) However, it seems to me more accurate to maintain that stereotype is just a widely shared hypothesis, as it were; it is what seems to us, on the surface, to warrant the assumption that the phenomena have something deeper in common, something that warrants rigid* designation of its extension. Depending on theories and further knowledge acquired about the hidden nature of the kind, the beliefs we have shared about the stereotypes may persist over time, or they may need to be revised. But as Putnam himself argued, none of these initial hypotheses is secure from possible revision as more knowledge accumulates about the real nature of the kind, including the possibility that we got the stereotype(s) wrong.[14]

The crucial question for us, however, is how much of this natural kinds model can be extended to cover other types of words or concepts, in particular evaluative terms, like justice, freedom, or equality, the kind of terms we find in constitutional documents. And that depends, you might think, on metaethics. Dworkin, for one, seems to be treating the main concepts of constitutional evaluative terms as if they were moral natural kinds.[15] Perry is also quite explicit that his view about the prohibition of "cruel" punishment in the Eighth

[12] H. Putnam, *Mind, Language and Reality* at 250.

[13] It is quite possible that different types of knowledge are required for using a word more or less correctly under some circumstances, and for what would count as understanding a word as used in a given idiolect. The differences, however, might be just a matter of degree.

[14] To be sure, I am not suggesting that the meaning of natural kind remains the same even if, over time, there are radical changes in the widely shared theories about the nature of its extension. I do not think that we have very robust intuitions about this.

[15] See, for example, his *Justice in Robes* at 154–56. A similar view is defended by David Brink, for example, in "Legal Theory, Legal Interpretation, and Judicial Review." Brink is a realist about moral terms, while Dworkin is not. See his "Objectivity and Truth." Dworkin's metaethical position is difficult to pin down. Basically, he aims to defend an objectivist position without metaphysical realism.

Amendment presupposes a kind of realism about moral terms; it assumes that certain things can turn out to be cruel, really cruel, even if people thought otherwise.[16] Granted, on the basis of an externalist or realist metaethics, construal of evaluative terms such as "cruel," "equal protection," etc., along the lines of natural kinds is plausible. And then, it seems, we would have the building blocks for the kind of dynamic reading of the Constitution that Dworkin and Perry espouse. We could say that the Constitution prohibits cruel punishments *rigidly**—namely, whatever is really cruel (viz., according to an externalist version of "is C"), which, practically speaking, is tantamount to whatever turns out to be cruel upon our best knowledge available at the time of interpretation.

There are several problems with this suggestion, however. First, even if we grant that, as a metaethical position, the externalist model is plausible, it does not necessarily settle the question about constitutional interpretation that we have been discussing here. Truth does not always settle the question of how to understand the law, just as truth does not always affect the content that parties to a conversation can convey to each other. As we saw in chapter 2, we can think of a conversation between A and B, both assuming that John is married to Susan, and in their conversation they refer to John as "Susan's husband." As it happens, the truth is that John and Susan are not legally married. Nevertheless, for all practical purposes, nothing is necessarily amiss in the conversation between A and B; they both refer to the person they want to refer to, they understand each other, and the content of the conversation is not necessarily affected by their false presupposition.

Consider a legal case now: in the curious case of *Nix v. Hedden*,[17] the question came up about whether tomatoes are fruit or vegetable. The law imposed a 10 percent duty on importation of vegetables, and exempted fruit from the tariff; the plaintiff, who imported tomatoes, claimed that tomatoes are actually fruit, not vegetable, and hence claimed the exemption. The court acknowledged that, as a matter of scientific taxonomy, tomatoes are, indeed, fruit and not vegetable. Nevertheless, the court decided that, for the purposes of determining the classification of tomatoes in the context of this law, the ordinary, albeit scientifically mistaken, understanding of people that tomatoes are vegetables is the correct reading of the statute. Didn't the court

[16] J. Perry, "Textualism and the Discovery of Rights" at 118ff.

[17] 149 U.S. 304 (1893).

realize that the relevant terms here are natural kinds, you might wonder? Well, it did, in a way (though not in these terms, of course); but the court reasoned, and quite sensibly, I think, that natural kind terms are not necessarily used as such, either in ordinary conversations or in legislation. Legislation is not a scientific theory, aiming to get to the truth of the matter about the real nature of things, so to speak. The law aims to regulate conduct for some particular purposes, and the pragmatics of legal utterances must take this into account. The law often relies on assumptions about how people normally understand certain words or concepts, even if those understandings are far from accurate or scientifically sound.

The *Nix v. Hedden* decision is not out of line with ordinary use of language in other contexts. Rigid* designation, of the kind Putnam explored in connection with natural kinds, is a tricky matter. In many cases, it depends on conversational purposes and a speaker's intentions. It is quite right that when natural kind words, such as "gold" or "tiger" or "water," are introduced into natural language, the collective intention of language users is to treat these words as natural kinds, rigidly* designating the extension, whatever it really is. But collective linguistic intention does not necessarily trump a speaker's intentions in concrete conversational contexts. Speakers often use words that are normally treated as natural kinds without intending to employ rigid* designation in the particular context of their utterance. When you order a fruit salad in a restaurant, you really do not expect to get tomatoes mixed in with the grapes, apples, and oranges; in this context the word "fruit" is not meant as a natural kind (technically speaking, that is), and the waiter would be rather obnoxious if he pretended to have understood you otherwise. In short, whether we use a natural kind word as rigidly* designating its extension or not often depends on the relevant interests and salient contextual features shared by parties to the conversation.

Dworkin and Perry could claim, however, that in the context of constitutional law, there are good reasons to treat the general moral terms in the Constitution as moral natural kinds. There are two possible arguments to that effect. One, which Dworkin has explicitly made, is linguistic. Dworkin argued that the very use of such general and abstract formulations as "*equal* protection of the laws" or "*cruel* and unusual punishment" is itself evidence of the *communication intention* of the framers to designate rigidly* whatever is the best understanding of the general moral terms. Had the framers wanted to avoid rigid* designation, they would have used much more concrete and specific language, as is normally done in the context of statutory law. So the argument seems to be that, in the specific context of enacting a constitution, the use of very general and abstract terms is decisive evidence of the communication intention of the framers—namely, the intention to use the general terms as moral natural kinds.[18]

This argument rests on shaky grounds, however. First, evidence about a speaker's intention is always defeasible; concrete historical evidence may disprove the hypothesis. Second, the heavy reliance on the actual communication intentions of the framers is a bit perplexing a position for Dworkin to hold. He has made it abundantly clear that in the context of statutory interpretation he would not regard communication intentions decisive of any interpretative issue—so why make it decisive in constitutional interpretation, where it is, morally speaking, much more problematic?[19] Most important, however, is that Dworkin's main assumption here is far from secure: people often use very general and abstract terms not intending to use them with rigid* designation, even if the terms are of natural kinds. It all depends on the presuppositions of the particular conversation in question—namely, on what is taken for granted by the speaker and assumed by the speaker to be taken for granted by the relevant audience.

The better argument for the conclusion that general moral terms in the Constitution should be understood on the basis of the natural kinds model is a moral one. It is certainly possible for Dworkin and Perry to argue that, regardless of actual communication intentions, there are moral–political reasons to treat the moral terms in the Constitution as rigidly* designating whatever is, actually, the right moral extension of the terms in question. I will explore what this argument might be in the last section. For now, let me just point out that, even if we think that the moral argument goes through, two additional problems remain.

First, the conclusion that general moral terms in a constitutional document should be understood on the basis of an externalist model ties the view about constitutional interpretation to some version of externalism in metaethics. The view only makes sense if we assume that moral terms rigidly* designate something that is out there, so to speak, regardless of our collective, widely shared conceptions of its

[18] See R. M. Dworkin, *Freedom's Law* at 7–12.

[19] I elaborated on this critique in greater detail in my *Interpretation and Legal Theory* (revised 2nd ed.), ch. 9.

nature. Perhaps it does not take a full-fledged version of realism in metaethics to make sense of such a view, but some version of externalism about moral concepts is clearly required.[20] The problem is that this may seem like a hefty price tag: do we really want a theory of constitutional interpretation that is tied to a particular metaethics, and one that is not uncontroversial, to put it mildly?

Second, and more importantly, perhaps, is that if we construe the relevant evaluative terms along the lines of natural kind predicates, the distinction between concept and conceptions becomes very problematic. If you assume that, say, "cruel" or "cruelty" is like a natural kind, rigidly* designating a moral kind, as it were, then you must assume that there is a truth of the matter about which conception of cruelty is the correct one (if any). On this view, competing conceptions of such concepts are akin to competing hypotheses or theories about the true nature of the extension, and therefore, if one of them is true, others, incompatible with it, must be false. But then the kind of conceptual tolerance we assumed about different conceptions of the same concept, far from being explained, is actually explained away; it turns out to be a mistake. Yet again, this is a hefty price tag for a theory of constitutional interpretation. It entails that rational people cannot have a reasonable disagreement about what, say, "equal protection of the laws" requires, any more than they can have a reasonable disagreement about the chemical composition of water.[21] Thus it turns out that the distinction between a concept and its different conceptions, employed by Dworkin and Perry to explain their views about constitutional interpretation, does not provide us with the tools to explain how people can reasonably disagree about their favored conceptions of the concept in question. On the externalist semantic model we explored here, such disagreements are, at least in principle, resolvable. Hence, if one conception is true, others, incompatible with it, must be discarded as false.[22] This makes sense as a model for

[20] Both Perry and Dworkin acknowledge this point, to some extent. See Dworkin, *Justice in Robes* at 154–7 and Perry, "Textualism and Discovery of Rights" at 123–25.

[21] Of course, disagreements about the chemical composition of water would have been perfectly rational before the discovery that water is composed of H_2O. But even then, it must have been assumed that opposing views on the issue could not be mutually consistent.

[22] Alternatively, one might hold a view that the concept in question refers to the kind of things that are out there, in some realist sense, but whose nature is essentially *unknowable*. In that case, disagreements between different conceptions are not, in principle, resolvable. But this would certainly not make the kind of disagreements we have about different conceptions more rational than the natural kind model does.

scientific disagreement, but not for a moral–political disagreement of the kind we find in constitutional interpretation.

3. The Internalist Model: Essentially Contested Concepts

The idea that rational people can have reasonable disagreements about their favored conception of an evaluative concept gives us a starting point for examining a very different approach, suggested by W. B. Gallie's influential article about *essentially contested concepts*.[23] As I hope to show here, this is the opposite approach to the externalist model that we considered above. According to Gallie, certain evaluative concepts—such as art, democracy, social justice, "a Christian way of life," and the like—exhibit a particularly strong version of what I have called conceptual tolerance. It is a strong version because people tend to hold different conceptions of the contested concept in way that is *essentially competitive*: people tend to think that their favored conception is superior to other people's, yet they also recognize that their conception is legitimately contested by others and in a way that is "not resolvable by argument of any kind."[24] So the picture we are presented with here is of a kind of competition of conceptions, each favored by some and rejected by others, exhibiting seemingly contradictory beliefs; people believe that they got it right and others got it wrong, but they also know that there is no decisive argument for resolving the controversy. Furthermore, Gallie's main point seems to be that these concepts are such that the competitive conceptions they engender are unavoidable; they are *essentially* contested, and do not just happen to be so in a particular context. Gallie employs a hypothetical sports competition to demonstrate his argument. The contested concept of the game that Gallie constructs exhibits five characteristic features:

(1) The concept in question must be *apprasive*, in that it stands for some kind of valued achievement.
(2) The achievement in question must be internally complex.
(3) The explanation of its worth must refer to the respective contribution of its parts or features.

[23] W. B. Gallie, *Proceedings of the Aristotelian Society* (1956), 167.
[24] Gallie, *Proceedings of the Aristotelian Society* (1956) at 169.

(4) The accredited achievement must be of a kind that admits of modifications in light of changing circumstances.
(5) Each party recognizes that its own understanding of the concept is contested by other parties.

Presumably, these five features are meant to help us see how certain evaluative concepts can be essentially contested—namely, how people can think that their conception is superior to other people's while acknowledging that they have no decisive argument to prove it, at least not in a way that would render a rejection of their argument irrational on the part of their competitors. Still, there is something rather curious about this. The complexity and interdependence of the various elements that make up the relevant concept are not enough to explain its essentially contested nature. There has to be more to it than that.

Now, we do have one familiar model of evaluative preferences, which enables people to have such preferences while acknowledging that others, who may disagree, do not have to share them. We call it "a matter of taste." I prefer French wine to the Californian wines, and I think that French wine is generally better, more true to the nature of red wine, as it were, than Californian wine, which, in my view, is too fruity and thus too artificial. But I do not really think that those who pay more money for a Californian wine are stupid or just plain wrong. This is, at least partly, a matter of taste (literally and figuratively, if you will). Generally speaking, we can say that preferences of taste are such that either we think that others do not have to share them with us, that there is no other-regarding "ought" in play here, or else, if there is some "ought" in play, the overall evaluation is at least partly subjective, at least partly a matter of some subjective preference, not necessarily a universal requirement applying to others similarly situated. Either way, the realization that the relevant evaluative concept in play is such that at least part of its components or constitutive features are a matter of taste makes it easy to understand how one's preferred conception is compatible with a strong form of conceptual tolerance.

Another explanation for the kind of conceptual tolerance that essentially contested concepts exhibit can be due to *incommensurability*. Suppose the constitutive elements that make up the evaluative concept are such that they are incommensurable with other elements. To give a schematic example, suppose it is generally believed that concept C, appraisive and all, is partly a matter of scoring high on dimensions *a*, *b*, and *c*. However, it is also the case that *a*, *b*, and *c* are incommensurable.

Thus, suppose we have two conceptions of C, C(1) and C(2), such that C(1) scores higher on *a* than C(2) but lower on *b*. If *a* and *b* are incommensurable, then we would have no exact sense of how much higher on *a* C(1) has to score to compensate for a lower score on *b* (and vice versa). And of course, this model can be made more complex with more elements in the overall evaluation, colliding and competing on various fronts. To give a concrete example: consider the differences between living in a big city and living in a small town. Each of these lifestyles has advantages and disadvantages on scores of evaluative dimensions. And, quite plausibly, some of these dimensions are incommensurable (e.g., how would you compare lengths of commute time with better theater? Or a certain level of pollution with better schools?). And this would certainly explain why the choice between living in a big city or a small town is "not resolvable by argument of any kind."

Now, the problem is that both explanations, taste and incommensurability, give us as sense of why it is difficult to settle an argument about the preference of C(1) over C(2); both explanations give us a sense of how people can adhere to competing conceptions of the same general evaluative concept. But neither explanation seems to give us an idea of why people have a particularly strong other-regarding preference for their favored conception. If C(1) and C(2) are incommensurably good (or bad), the rational reaction in the face of disagreement should be one of evaluative indifference, not competition. In short, neither taste-based nor incommensurability-based explanations (or any combination of both) gives us the right sort of contestability here.

In order to get the right kind of contestability, we probably need to take Gallie's game/sports analogy more seriously: we get a competition when a winner has to be declared. More broadly, we can say that when a decision has to be reached, collectively, institutionally, or authoritatively, about which conception gets implemented in a given context or, at least, which one is somehow declared the winner, then we are likely to get the kind of strong contestability that Gallie had in mind. Indeed, all the examples that Gallie mentions have this element: in matters of justice we need to make collective, often authoritative decisions; indifference or abstention of judgment is often not an option, practically speaking. Similarly, about questions regarding the nature of democracy, what counts as "truly" democratic and the like, decisions are often practically needed. Art may seem like an example where declaring a winner is not quite required, but that's not accurate. For various practical purposes, such as public recognition, financial support, market price, etc., various collectives and institutions do need to declare winners and losers. And so on and so forth.

Does this mean that competition between conceptions exists where it really should not be present? Is it Gallie's suggestion here that essentially contested concepts exhibit a kind of cognitive overreach? Undoubtedly, there are cases in which the practical need, or perceived need, to declare a winner generates distortions, pushing people to believe that their conception of an essentially contested concept is superior to other people's, while the simple truth might be that it is nothing more than a complex subjective preference (at least in part). How much we want to generalize this diagnostic explanation is, of course, a very complex issue that lies at the heart of some of the most contentious theories in metaethics and related philosophical debates. I will not pursue this question here. Instead, I want to explore some of the linguistic background further, getting us back to the question we started with.

4. Super-Polysemy and the Pragmatics of Conceptions

Remember that we started with a puzzle about the relations between meaning and beliefs. The question we were interested in is about the possibility of sharing the meaning of a general concept-word while disagreeing, sometimes profoundly, about what the word stands for, about the essential characteristics of its extension. The externalist model gave us one plausible account of how convergence in meaning is compatible with disagreements about the extension of the word. Gallie's theory about essentially contested concepts gave us an internalist account; it purports to explain the disagreements about the extension of a concept-word in terms of the internal complexities of the constitutive elements of the relevant concept and the speakers' subjective judgments or preferences about the relations between them. The important point to realize is that both models work at the general semantic level; they tell us something about the ways we normally think about relations between meaning and the extension of different types of words/concepts. In concrete contexts of speech, however, pragmatic factors may yield different results.

We have already seen that natural kind words can be used by speakers in a particular context of speech without intending to refer to the extension of the word rigidly*. But now we should see that this is just an example of a much more general phenomenon: the intended reference or extension of words used in a given conversation is often sensitive to context and other pragmatic determinants of linguistic communication. In chapter 5, we discussed the general phenomenon of polysemy, whereby the same nonambiguous word would be used to designate different extensions, depending on the context of the expression and shared presuppositions, or background knowledge, about the world.

This sensitivity to context of expressions in designating extension is ubiquitous, and applies to evaluative terms as well—in fact, often much more so. The kind of evaluative concept-words we have in the constitutional context may well be called *super-polysemy.* These are the kind of evaluative concept-words that can be used to refer to different kinds of concerns, often only vaguely related to each other, and hugely depending on context of expression. Consider, for example, the concept of fairness. Suppose somebody utters the expression:

"It is not fair that X..."

Now consider the following options for X:

(a) My daughter saying, "You bought my sister a new shirt but not me."
(b) The president saying, "The most wealthy people in the country pay such low rates of income tax."
(c) The inmate in prison saying, "I got convicted, but I didn't do it."
(d) My wife saying, "We planned this trip for so long and now the weather is going to ruin it."

Clearly the words "not fair" stand for rather different kinds of concerns here. In (a) there is some notion of equal treatment in play; in (b) there is some notion of redistribution in play; in (c) it is a concern about truth and desert; and in (d) it is about bad luck. Of course, under normal conditions, we can easily discern these differences of intended extension and they pose no particular problems in ordinary conversation. Problems arise when the intended extension depends on more complex beliefs and presuppositions that are not quite as transparent in the conversational situation in play. Then, if we try to clarify the relevant presuppositions, we may sometimes discover that we have been talking past each other. At other times, of course, we may reach bedrock upon realizing that we simply disagree about fundamental questions of value.

Here is another example, closer to the constitutional context: many people believe that there is too much cruelty involved in some of the penal practices currently prevalent in the U.S. Such people have serious reservations about the excessive cruelty of exceedingly long prison terms, often in harsh conditions, inflicted on offenders, and many think that capital punishment is cruel and unjustified. Now compare the reference of "cruel" in these two cases: excessive prison terms and capital punishment. Upon reflection, it should be clear that speakers use the word "cruel" to refer to different kinds of concerns. Long prison terms are cruel, if they are, in a fairly standard sense of the word—namely, one designating the infliction of too much harm or suffering that is not necessary under the circumstances. But if you ask people whether this is also their main concern about capital punishment, my guess is that most people would say *no*. Their moral objection to capital punishment does not consist in the concern that the act of killing inflicts too much suffering on the condemned.[25] The moral concerns pertain to other aspects of capital punishment, such as the irreversibility of it, which is extremely troubling given the possibility of error in conviction; its racially biased application; the concern that the state should not be in the business of taking away human life; and so on. In short, cruelty about capital punishment refers to something quite different from cruelty about long prison terms. Think about it this way: in response to concerns about harsh and long prison terms, it makes sense to retort, "They deserve it"—it would be a relevant (albeit probably misguided) reaction. But in response to the main concerns about capital punishment, "They deserve it" is the wrong kind of response. Many of those who object to capital punishment would not deny that heinous murderers may deserve to die; what they are concerned about is the risk of error, racism, the role of the state in making it the case that this kind of desert is implemented, and similar considerations.[26]

[25] Killing can be swift and painless, though somehow states manage to fail to make this so. Of course, that's not the main concern here.

[26] I can see an objection to the example: one might argue that people couch their objection to capital punishment in terms of cruelty only because of the language of the Eighth Amendment, and not because they think that cruelty is really an issue here. Well, yes, it is quite possible that this is the case now in the U.S., but I would venture to guess that cruelty was an issue with capital punishment in European countries when those

In short, general evaluative concepts are typically *super-polysemous*; such concept-words have a very wide semantic range, and they tend to designate different types of concerns, depending on context, background assumptions, the speaker's intention, etc. But now, if you think about constitutional documents, you can see that polysemy is a major concern, and not only because it plagues general evaluative terms of the kind deployed in constitutional documents. The main problem in the constitutional case is the *essentially thin conversational context*: constitutions do not form part of an ordinary conversation between parties sharing a great deal of background contextual knowledge. After all, the main purpose of constitutions is to regulate conduct on a large scale, in very general terms, for generations to come. It is not anything like an intimate conversation between parties situated in a particular context; the conversational context of constitutional provisions is inevitably very thin.

Now, you might think that the thin conversational background of constitutional enactments vindicates the Dworkin–Perry position; it shows that understanding general constitutional provisions in all but their most abstract terms is inevitable, because we lack the kind of conversational background, and other pragmatic determinates of communicated content, that we would normally have in an ordinary conversation. In other words, we can reinterpret the Dworkin–Perry argument to say that the mistake of originalism is precisely in dealing with constitutional enactment as if it was an ordinary conversation, where we can construe the intended extension of words used by relying on the normal pragmatic determinants, whereas, in fact, there are no such pragmatic factors in play. Though this line of thought is in the right direction, it is still rather precarious. Originalists could reply that nothing is said entirely out of context. Even if the conversational context of constitutional enactments is relatively thin, some context is surely there, and sometimes, at least, is essential for understanding what the Constitution says.

Consider, for example, the formulation in the Eighth Amendment of the prohibition on inflicting "cruel and unusual" punishment. This is an ambiguous expression: does it mean that a form of punishment would be unconstitutional only if it is both cruel *and* unusual, or if it is either cruel *or* unusual? Logicians would tell you that "P & Q"

countries debated the issue and decided to abolish capital punishment. But not much hangs on this; other, similar examples are abundant.

is true if and only if P is true and Q is true, and false if either one is false. But now suppose you see a sign on the entrance to a store saying "No dogs and cats allowed"—surely the sign is not meant to keep out only those patrons who happen to have both a dog *and* a cat, but either one. The opposite is true of a sign saying, "No drinking and driving"—it is not meant to suggest that either drinking or driving is prohibited, only the combination of the two. This familiar type of scope ambiguity is normally resolved by contextual or background knowledge of the parties to the conversation. You cannot infer the right conclusion from the meaning of the expression alone. So there is something about context we must know in order to interpret the "cruel and unusual" punishment prohibition; the semantics of conjunction would not give us the answer.

To be sure, I am not trying to defend originalism here. I think that Dworkin's position is much more plausible from a moral point of view. But in order to get to it, we need a moral–political argument, not a linguistic one. The way we think about the linguistic framework of constitutional documents depends on the moral–political framework, not the other way around. Let me explain what I mean here.

5. The Moral Debate and the Nature of the Conversation

Constitutions are, by their very nature, *precommitment* devices. When a legal system adopts a constitution, especially one that is fairly "rigid" (as the U.S. Constitution certainly is), the legal system basically precommits to certain principles of governance and certain moral–political principles that are deliberately made difficult to change by the ordinary democratic process of legislation. Like Ulysses who ties himself to the mast and, crucially, orders his subordinates to ignore his future orders, in order to prevent the possibility of succumbing to irresistible temptation in the future, constitutions tie the nation to the mast, striving to make it difficult to succumb to some future temptations. The question of what makes this precommitment device legitimate, especially in the face of its essentially anti-democratic or at least anti-majoritarian element, is the central question about the legitimacy of constitutionalism. Neither Dworkin nor Scalia purports to provide us with an elaborate answer to this question. But it is clear that they have very different views about it, and that they understand the precommitment aspect of constitutionalism very differently.

According to Scalia, the whole point of entrenching certain moral–political principles in a rigid constitutional document is to freeze those principles in time, as it were. It is, after all, the whole point of a constitutional regime to predetermine certain issues, controversial as they may become, and freeze a certain resolution to those issues in time, for generations to come. Not a total freeze, of course; constitutions provide for their own amendment process and can be changed accordingly. But the amendments are not easy to accomplish, precisely because their whole point is to function as a counter-majoritarian element in the legal system, making it difficult to change by the ordinary democratic processes. Therefore, Scalia concludes, it is incumbent on interpreters of the Constitution to defer to an "original" understanding of its content, because this is the whole point of the precommitment to constitutional constraints. If we do not like those ideas then we need to amend the Constitution. Allowing judges to adapt the Constitution to current moral–political conceptions, thus circumventing the burdensome amendment process, would be tantamount to subverting the very idea of constitutionalism as an anti-majoritarian precommitment device. This, I submit, is quite simply the main idea behind originalism in constitutional interpretation.[27]

Those, like Dworkin, who favor a much more dynamic version of constitutional interpretation, obviously disagree; they see the precommitment element of a constitutional regime as much more limited. Why is that? Presumably, because there is something deeply problematic about the very idea of an intergenerational precommitment of the kind imposed on us by rigid constitutions. It is far from obvious that any one generation should have the moral authority to bind future generations to its conceptions of the just and the good. But to some extent, this is precisely what constitutions do, and inevitably so. They bind future generations to the mast, making certain decisions

[27] See A. Scalia, *A Matter of Interpretation* at 37–47. This main rationale needs many further refinements and adaptations, of course. For example, even if we are totally committed to an original understanding of a constitutional provision, borderline cases of vague terms might not be contextually determined, and judicial precisification of such vague terms may be needed. Even the most dogmatic version of originalism must allow for some judicial innovation in the face of changing circumstances and relatively thin contextual information. I am told by constitutional lawyers that this is now called "construction," as opposed to "interpretation." In their terminology, originalism concedes, as it must, that some constitutional construction is necessary. Well, quite a bit, I would say.

about morality and politics much more difficult to accomplish than would normally be allowed by an ordinary democratic process. This intergenerational authority is morally problematic, to say the least, and its legitimacy is far from evident. And, of course, the more we regard constitutional content as tied to its original understanding, the more acute the problem of legitimacy becomes. Therefore, allowing the Supreme Court to adapt the content of the Constitution to current understandings of its main moral–political principles is a means of mitigating the intergenerational concern.

I will not pretend to have made any philosophical news here; these fundamental problems about the legitimacy of a rigid constitutional regime are well known and their implications well understood. The suggestion I would like to make concerns the ways in which we should think about the linguistic considerations that bear on this debate. What I have tried to show is that the protagonists to the debate got the direction wrong here. They conduct the argument as if the linguistic considerations about the concept versus conceptions distinction can be utilized to support their moral–political views about the rationale of a constitutional regime and its moral legitimacy. But, in fact, it is exactly the other way around. The moral–political views about the rationale of a rigid constitutional regime are the ones that should inform the ways in which we think about what kind of speech act constitutional documents are, and the kind of conversation that constitutions establish.

Why so? If you think that the intergenerational precommitment embodied in a rigid constitutional framework is legitimate, as originalists clearly do, then you would be quite right to regard the constitutional document as an ordinary legislative speech act, whereby the framers of the Constitution purport to communicate some definite legal content, and it is our task to try to figure out what that content is. In other words, according to the moral–political view shared by originalists, it makes sense to think about the Constitution as a legislative speech act in a conversation between framers and subjects, just as we think about ordinary legislation as a conversation in which the legislature says something and we try to understand what the legislature actually said (and perhaps also what it implicated or presupposed, etc.). In other words, the more you agree with the precommitment rationale of constitutionalism, the more you would be inclined to think about the constitutional document as a product of an ordinary legislative speech act that purports to communicate certain contents that we need to ascertain. And vice versa, of course. The more doubtful you are, morally speaking, about the precommitment rationale of a constitutional regime, and, in particular, the more concerned you are about the intergenerational authority of a rigid constitution, the less you would be inclined to think about the Constitution as a legislative speech act. The general constitutional provisions containing abstract moral–political principles, according to this view, might be seen as a kind of vague and general framework, setting the language and the general terms in which moral–political concerns need to be legally phrased, but leaving the content of the relevant expressions free for the courts to shape as they deem right at any given time. Thus, the real debate here is about the nature of the conversation that our constitutional regime establishes, which depends on our views about the rationale of constitutionalism, what constitutions are for, and what makes them legitimate.

An objection needs to be answered before we conclude the discussion: the nature of the conversation, one might think, is typically determined by the speaker. What kind of conversation one engages in is not usually an open question, and typically not one for the hearer to determine. It is, normally, the speaker who gets to set the terms of the conversation, as it were. Whether something has been said as a straightforward proposition, or in jest, or ironically, or fictitiously, are matters that depend on the speaker's intention. If that is correct, one might resist the idea that there is room for a moral–political debate about the nature of the conversation that constitutions establish; one might think that we are forced to side with the originalists and maintain that it is up to the framers and their communication intention to set the terms of the relevant type of conversation in question here.

This objection can be answered without too many difficulties. Though generally true that it is the speaker who gets to determine the nature of the conversation, it is not always the case and not necessarily so. In some cases, the nature of the conversation is partly determined by the hearer, not the speaker. A clear example, though perhaps not very close to our concerns here, is a typical conversation between patient and psychologist, whereby the patient tells a story, from a certain autobiographical perspective, and the psychologist registers something else, not so much the content conveyed but the reasons or hidden motives for conveying it, the kind of things the content conveyed tells about the patient and his or her problems, etc. A session with a psychologist (or a conversation with a friend who wants to be your psychologist on that occasion) is one clear example where the speaker does not get to determine the kind of conversation that actually takes place.

Another example, and much closer to our concerns, obtains in the kind of cases where authors speak to multiple audiences, situated in different contexts and often spanning different times and places. The main example, of course, is literature and other, similar forms of art. It is a very familiar point that the ways in which we understand literature is partly a matter of aesthetic and artistic judgment exercised by the readers, irrespective, at least to some extent, of the intentions of the authors. In other words, it is part of our very conception of literature that the speaker/author does not necessarily get to determine, as it were, what exactly is the nature of the conversation she conducts with her readers. What kind of conversation takes place between authors and readers in the case of literature is an open question, never entirely determined by the relevant authors. In this respect, constitutional law is much closer to literature than one might have thought. In both cases, the nature of the conversation is partly up to the readers, not the authors, to determine. And in both cases, different ways of understanding the nature of the conversation reflect different evaluative views about the nature of the enterprise and the kind of values we find in it.

If this argument looks like the kind of argument Dworkin himself should have made, the impression is not mistaken. I have long argued that one of Dworkin's best insights about the nature of interpretation concerns the ways in which evaluative views about the nature of the genre, or the relevant enterprise, necessarily inform any particular interpretative views within it. Without having some views about the main values we find in the genre to which the object we strive to interpret belongs—its main point or rationale, as it were—it is almost impossible to say anything about what would count as an acceptable interpretation. You cannot begin to offer an interpretation of a novel if you have no views about what makes novels good and worthy of our appreciation. Similarly, I do not see how one can have any theories about constitutional interpretation that are not responsive to one's moral–political theory about the rationale of constitutionalism and the moral legitimacy of judicial review. Had Dworkin followed his own line of thought here, there would have been no need on his part to rely on the kind of linguistic and historical considerations that his arguments about constitutional interpretation deployed over the years. One can only surmise that Dworkin wanted to defeat the originalists on their own turf. But that does not work, and it only obscures the true nature of the debate, which is, as Dworkin should have been the first to note, essentially a moral-political debate about what constitutions are for and what makes them legitimate to begin with.

Bibliography

Austin, J. L. (1962) *How to Do Things with Words*, 2nd ed., J. O. Urmson and M. Sbisà, eds., Cambridge, MA: Harvard University Press.

Bach, K. (2005) "Context *ex Machina*," in Z. G. Szabó, ed., *Semantics versus Pragmatics*, Oxford: Oxford University Press, pp. 15–44.

Bach, K. and Harnish, R. M. (1992) "How Performatives Really Work: A Reply to Searle," *Linguistics and Philosophy* 15(1): 93–110.

Bach, K. and Harnish, R. M. (1982) *Linguistic Communication and Speech Acts*, Cambridge, MA: The MIT Press.

Brink, D. O. (1988) "Legal Theory, Legal Interpretation, and Judicial Review," *Philosophy & Public Affairs* 17(2): 105–48.

Byrne, A. (1993) "Truth in Fiction: The Story Continued," *Australasian Journal of Philosophy* 71(1): 25–35.

Carston, R. A. (2013) "Legal Texts and Canons of Construction: A View from Current Pragmatic Theory," in M. Freeman and F. Smith, eds., *Law and Language: Current Legal Issues, Vol. 15*, Oxford: Oxford University Press, pp. 8–33.

Carston, R. A. (2004) "Explicature and Semantics," in S. Davis and B. S. Gillon, eds., *Semantics: A Reader*, Oxford: Oxford University Press, pp. 817–45.

Chomsky, C. (2011) "The Story of *Holy Trinity Church v. United States* (1892): Spirit and History in Statutory Interpretation," in W. N. Eskridge, Jr., P. P. Frickey, and E. Garrett, eds., *Statutory Interpretation Stories*, New York: Thomson Reuters/Foundation Press, pp. 2–35.

Conan Doyle, A. (1892) "The Adventure of the Speckled Band," in *The Adventures of Sherlock Holmes*, London: George Newnes Ltd.

Dan-Cohen, M. (2002) "Decision Rules and Conduct Rules: On Acoustic Separation in Criminal Law," in *Harmful Thoughts: Essays on Law, Self, and Morality*, Princeton, NJ: Princeton University Press, pp. 37–93.

Dan-Cohen, M. (1995) "Interpreting Official Speech," in A. Marmor, ed., *Law and Interpretation: Essays in Legal Philosophy*, Oxford: Hart Publishing, pp. 433–50.

Donnellan, K. S. (1966) "Reference and Definite Descriptions," *The Philosophical Review* 77: 281–304.

Dworkin, R. M. (2006) *Justice in Robes*, Cambridge, MA: Harvard University Press.

Dworkin, R. M. (1997) "Comment," in A. Scalia, *A Matter of Interpretation: Federal Courts and the Law*, A. Gutman, ed., Princeton, NJ: Princeton University Press, pp. 115–28.

Dworkin, R. M. (1996) *Freedom's Law: The Moral Reading of the American Constitution*, Cambridge, MA: Harvard University Press.

Dworkin, R. M. (1996) "Objectivity and Truth: You'd Better Believe It," *Philosophy and Public Affairs 25*: 87–139.

Dworkin, R. M. (1986) *Law's Empire*, Cambridge, MA: Belknap Press of Harvard University Press.

Ekins, R. (2012) *The Nature of Legislative Intent*, Oxford: Oxford University Press.

Endicott, T. (2011) "The Value of Vagueness," in A. Marmor and S. Soames, eds., *Philosophical Foundations of Language in the Law*, Oxford: Oxford University Press, pp. 14–30.

Endicott, T. (2002) "Law and Language," in E. N. Zalta, ed., *The Stanford Encyclopedia of Philosophy*, <http://plato.stanford.edu/archives/win2002/entries/law-language>.

Fuller, L. L. (1964) *The Morality of Law*, New Haven, CT: Yale University Press.

Fuller, L. L. (1958) "Positivism and Fidelity to Law: A Reply to Professor Hart," *Harvard Law Review 71*: 630.

Gallie, W. B. (1956) "Essentially Contested Concepts," *Proceedings of the Aristotelian Society 56*: 167–98.

Greenberg, M. (2011) "Legislation as Communication? Legal Interpretation and the Study of Linguistic Communication," in A. Marmor and S. Soames, eds., *Philosophical Foundations of Language in the Law*, Oxford: Oxford University Press, pp. 217–56.

Grice, P. (1989) *Studies in the Way of Words*, Cambridge, MA: Harvard University Press.

Hart, H. L. A. (1961) *The Concept of Law*, Oxford: Clarendon Press.

Hart, H. L. A. (1958) "Positivism and the Separation of Law and Morals," *Harvard Law Review 71*(4): 593–629.

Hart, H. M. and Sacks, A. M. (1994/1958) *The Legal Process: Basic Problems in the Making and Application of Law*, W. N. Eskridge and P. P. Frickey, eds., New York: Thomson Reuters/Foundation Press.

Jorgensen, J. (1937) "Imperatives and Logic," *Erkenntnis 7*: 288–96.

Kaplan, D. (1989) "Demonstratives: An Essay on the Semantics, Logic, Metaphysics, and Epistemology of Demonstratives and Other Indexicals," in J. Almog, J. Perry, and H. Wettstein, eds., *Themes from Kaplan*, Oxford: Oxford University Press, pp. 481–564.

Karttunen, L. and Peters, S. (1979) "Conventional Implicature," in *Syntax and Semantics, Vol. 11: Presupposition*, C. K. Oh and D. A. Dinneen, eds., New York: Academic Press, pp. 1–56.

Kelsen, H. (1967/1960) *Pure Theory of Law*, 2nd ed., M. Knight (trans.), Berkeley, CA: University of California Press.

King, J. C. and Stanley, J. (2005) "Semantics, Pragmatics, and the Role of Semantic Content," in Z. G. Szabó, ed., *Semantics versus Pragmatics*, Oxford: Oxford University Press, pp. 111–64.

Kripke, S. (2009) "Presupposition and Anaphora: Remarks on the Formulation of the Projection Problem," *Linguistic Inquiry 40*: 367–86.

Kripke, S. (1977) "Speaker's Reference and Semantic Reference," *Midwest Studies in Philosophy 2*(1): 255–76.

Lemmon, E. J. (1962) "On Sentences Verifiable by Their Use," *Analysis 22*(4): 86–89.

Lewis, D. K. (1983) "Truth in Fiction," in *Philosophical Papers, Vol. 1*, Oxford: Oxford University Press, pp. 261–75.

Manning, J. F. (2006) "What Divides Textualists from Purposivists?" *Columbia Law Review 106*(1): 70–111.

Marmor, A. (2013) "Farewell to Conceptual Analysis (in Jurisprudence)," in W. Waluchow and S. Sciaraffa, eds., *Philosophical Foundations of the Nature of Law*, Oxford: Oxford University Press, pp. 209–29.

Marmor, A. (2013) "Truth in Law," in M. Freeman and F. Smith, eds., *Law and Language: Current Legal Issues, Vol. 15*, Oxford: Oxford University Press, pp. 45–61.

Marmor, A. (2013) "Varieties of Vagueness in the Law," in G. Sartor, et al., eds., *Handbook of Legal Reasoning and Argumentation*, Dordrecht: Springer.

Marmor, A. (2011) "Can the Law Imply More than It Says? On Some Pragmatic Aspects of Strategic Speech," in A. Marmor and S. Soames, eds., *Philosophical Foundations of Language in the Law*, Oxford: Oxford University Press, pp. 83–104.

Marmor, A. (2010) *Philosophy of Law*, Princeton, NJ: Princeton University Press.

Marmor, A. (2009) *Social Conventions: From Language to Law*, Princeton, NJ: Princeton University Press.

Marmor, A. (2008) "The Pragmatics of Legal Language," *Ratio Juris 21*(4): 423–52.

Marmor, A. (2005) *Interpretation and Legal Theory* (revised 2nd ed.), Oxford: Hart Publishing.

McCubbins, M. D. and Rodriguez, D. B. (2005) "Canonical Construction and Statutory Revisionism: The Strange Case of the Appropriations Canon," *Journal of Contemporary Legal Issues 14*(2): 669–715.

Moore, M. (1981) "The Semantics of Judging," *Southern California Law Review 54*(2): 256–70.

Neale, S. "Textualism with Intent," unpublished ms, available at <http://www.ucl.ac.uk/laws/jurisprudence/docs/2008/08_coll_neale.pdf>.

Perry, J. (2011) "Textualism and the Discovery of Rights," in A. Marmor and S. Soames, eds., *Philosophical Foundations of Language in the Law*, Oxford: Oxford University Press, pp. 105–29.

Putnam, H. (1975) *Mind, Language and Reality: Philosophical Papers, Vol. 2*, Cambridge: Cambridge University Press.

Rawls, J. (1971) *A Theory of Justice*, Cambridge, MA: Belknap Press of Harvard University Press.

Raz, J. (2009) *Between Authority and Interpretation: On the Theory of Law and Practical Reason*, Oxford: Oxford University Press.

Raz, J. (1979) *The Authority of Law: Essays on Law and Morality*, Oxford: Oxford University Press.

Recanati, F. (1994) "Contextualism and Anti-Contextualism in the Philosophy of Language," in S. Tsohatzidis, ed., *Foundations of Speech Act Theory: Philosophical and Linguistic Perspectives*, London: Routledge, pp. 156–66.

Rodriguez, D. B. and Weingast, B. R. (2003) "The Positive Political Theory of Legislative History: New Perspectives on the 1964 Civil Rights Act and Its Interpretation," *University of Pennsylvania Law Review* 151(4): 1442–48.

Ryle, G. (1954) *Dilemmas*, Cambridge: Cambridge University Press.

Salmon, N. (2005) "Two Conceptions of Semantics," in Z. G. Szabó, ed., *Semantics versus Pragmatics*, Oxford: Oxford University Press, pp. 317–28.

Scalia, A. (1997) *A Matter of Interpretation: Federal Courts and the Law*, A. Gutman, ed., Princeton, NJ: Princeton University Press.

Scalia, A. and Garner, B. (2012) *Reading Law: The Interpretation of Legal Texts*, St. Paul, MN: Thomson/West.

Searle, J. R. (1979) *Expression and Meaning: Studies in the Theory of Speech Acts*, Cambridge: Cambridge University Press.

Shapiro, S. (2011) *Legality*, Cambridge, MA: Belknap Press of Harvard University Press.

Soames, S. (2012) "Vagueness and the Law," in A. Marmor, ed., *The Routledge Companion to Philosophy of Law*, New York: Routledge, pp. 95–108.

Soames, S. (2009) *Philosophical Essays, Vol. 2: The Philosophical Significance of Language*, Princeton, NJ: Princeton University Press.

Soames, S. (2008) *Philosophical Essays, Vol. 1: Natural Language: What It Means and How We Use It*, Princeton, NJ: Princeton University Press.

Sperber, D. and Wilson, D. (1986) *Relevance: Communication and Cognition*, Oxford: Blackwell.

Strawson, P. F. (1971) "Intention and Convention in Speech Acts," in *Logico-Linguistic Papers*, Aldershot: Ashgate, pp. 115–30.

Vermeule, A. (2006) *Judging Under Uncertainty: An Institutional Theory of Legal Interpretation*, Cambridge, MA: Harvard University Press.

Waldron, J. (2011) "Vagueness and the Guidance of Action," in A. Marmor and S. Soames, eds., *Philosophical Foundations of Language in the Law*, Oxford: Oxford University Press, pp. 58–82.

Waldron, J. (1999) *Law and Disagreement*, Oxford: Oxford University Press.

Walton, K. L. (1993) *Mimesis as Make-Believe: On the Foundations of the Representational Arts*, Cambridge, MA: Harvard University Press.

Williamson, T. (1994) *Vagueness*, London: Routledge.

Yaffe, G. (2010) *Attempts: In the Philosophy of Action and the Criminal Law*, Oxford: Oxford University Press.

Index

The manufacturer's authorised representative in the EU for product safety is Oxford University Press España S.A. of el Parque Empresarial San Fernando de Henares, Avenida de Castilla, 2 – 28830 Madrid (www.oup.es/en or product.safety@oup.com). OUP España S.A. also acts as importer into Spain of products made by the manufacturer.

www.ingramcontent.com/pod-product-compliance
Ingram Content Group UK Ltd.
Pitfield, Milton Keynes, MK11 3LW, UK
UKHW020923170926
475595UK00031B/33
* 9 7 8 0 1 9 8 7 1 4 5 3 8 *